RELIGIOUS STUDIES

GCSE Grade Booster

C. M. Jones
A. Jordan
A. Trotter

Schofield & Sims Ltd.

0 7217 4620 9

First printed 1992

Schofield & Sims Ltd.
Dogley Mill
Fenay Bridge
Huddersfield
HD8 0NQ
England

Typeset by Ocean, Leeds
Printed in England by the Alden Press, Oxford

Contents

SECTION 1: Christianity as a World Religion

Introduction

Christianity is the religion founded upon the life and teachings of Jesus Christ. This section of the book concentrates on the main beliefs and practices of Christianity as a world religion, in particular the three main divisions of the Christian Church – the Orthodox, Roman Catholic and Protestant traditions.

1 Christian Beliefs

Creeds

A creed is a statement of something people believe in. The word comes from the Latin *credo*, meaning 'I believe'.

The Church's first creed was 'Jesus Christ is Lord' (Romans 10,9; Philippians 2,11). For the earliest Christians this was sufficient, but as Christianity spread, a more detailed statement was needed. By the second century AD, one statement had increased to twenty, which became known a century later as the Apostles' Creed.

The Apostles' Creed

The Apostles' Creed sums up what the apostles taught:
I believe in God
  the Father Almighty,
  Maker of heaven and earth:
And in Jesus Christ
  His only Son our Lord,
  Who was conceived by the Holy Ghost,
  Born of the Virgin Mary,
  Suffered under Pontius Pilate
  Was crucified, dead, and buried;
  He descended into hell;
  The third day he rose again from the dead;
  He ascended into heaven,
  And sitteth on the right hand of God the Father Almighty;
  From thence he shall come to judge the quick and the dead.
I believe in
  The Holy Ghost;
  The Holy Catholic Church
  The Communion of Saints
  The forgiveness of sins;
  The resurrection of the body;
  and the life everlasting. Amen.

The creed falls into three parts.

1. The nature of God. For a Christian, the existence of God is a fact. The evidence is all around. God is the Supreme Being who has created the Universe and everything in it, including mankind. Though all-powerful, God is a Father who loves His Creation.

2. The importance of Jesus. God sent Jesus Christ, His only Son, to live as a man and to die for the sins of the world. Now risen from the dead, Jesus lives on in the presence of God. He will return to judge all people according to their actions and beliefs when they lived on earth.

3. The power of the Holy Spirit. God's work in the world continues through the power of the Holy Spirit. The Church is the holy, worldwide body of Christian people. Through belief in Jesus, individual Christians can be forgiven their sins. After death, they, too, will live on with God for ever.

The Apostles' Creed is still recited or sung by many Christians as part of their regular worship. There are two other creeds – the Nicene Creed and the Athanasian Creed. These are longer and more detailed than the Apostles' Creed.

• The Apostles' Creed is the Church's basic statement of belief: it makes clear what may be taught and what may be preached.

God

Christians believe that no one can *understand* God completely. Words are inadequate, but they do help people to *know* God.

For a Christian, God is:

• **One God.** That is to say, one as opposed to many.
• **Creator.** The universe is God's creation.
He is – pre-existent (has always been there)
        – omnipotent (all-powerful)
        – omnipresent (present everywhere)
        – omniscient (all-knowing).
• **Lord of All.** He is the master and ruler over all.
• **Father.** He is to be approached in prayer as a father (the *Lord's* Prayer: Matthew 6,9-13).
• **Judge.** He has made certain rules for people to live by. Disobedience will not go unpunished.

Jesus

Christians believe that Jesus was a historical figure who actually lived.

There is no known contemporary archaeological evidence of his life. The earliest known portrait of Jesus is in the catacombs of Rome and dates from AD 150.

The most important source of evidence is the written word. What written evidence there is, suggests strongly that Jesus was indeed a historical figure. There is a near-contemporary record of the crucifixion in the Annals of the Roman historian Tacitus. Jesus is mentioned in connection with trouble in Rome by another Roman writer, Suetonius. The first-century Jewish historian Josephus mentions Jesus, John the Baptist, Pontius Pilate and others who appear in the New Testament.

Our principal sources are the accounts in the four Gospels. There is no clear date for the birth of Jesus. According to Luke's Gospel, it was probably about the middle of the reign of the emperor Augustus (31 BC-AD 14). Augustus's successor Tiberius (AD 14-37) is mentioned in New Testament incidents connected with Jesus (e.g. Mark 12,13-17).

For most Christians, this evidence has been sufficient.

The Christian's View of Jesus

While he was alive, Jesus's disciples came to realise that he was someone special. They had expected a Messiah – a nationalist leader sent from God who would save his chosen people, the Jews, from their burden of foreign rule. Peter recognised Jesus as the true Messiah sent from God, who would save all people from their burden of sin.

After Jesus's death, his followers believed that God had raised him to life and that he had returned to heaven. Gradually, these followers, who became known as Christians, started to believe special things about Jesus. They gave him titles accordingly:

Lord

They began to call Jesus 'Lord' because they believed he shared in God's Lordship and power over all creation.

Son of God

Early Christians believed that when they saw Jesus they saw the true nature of God. By what is known as the *Incarnation*, God had come to life as a human being. Christians still believe that Jesus was fully man and fully God.

Jesus spoke of God as 'Father', so his first followers began to call him 'Son of God'. They believed he had a special relationship with God.

Redeemer

Christians call Jesus the 'Redeemer of the World'. People needed to be *redeemed* (delivered from sin) because they had broken God's laws and so had become separated from God. Traditional Christian teaching says people cannot make amends for their own sin. Only Jesus could make the perfect sacrifice and save all people. There were two reasons for this:

● Jesus is God, and so is the perfect sacrifice.

● Jesus is man, and can represent humanity when he offers his life in exchange for the sins of the world.

The price he paid to redeem people was his death on the cross. By this Christians are freed from sin and from the everlasting spiritual death of exile from God. This is known as *atonement*: Jesus atoned (made amends) for the sins of all people.

Saviour

The word Jesus means 'God saves'. To Christians, Jesus is 'Saviour'. They believe that Jesus brings salvation from injustice and also from sin, and that in his death he has saved anyone who believes in him from the punishment they deserve for their sins.

● This is one of the most important Christian beliefs, that humans cannot save themselves but that God has provided a way of salvation through Jesus.

Christ

The word Christ, used with the name Jesus, is really a title. It is a Greek translation of the Hebrew word Messiah, meaning 'anointed one'.

Son of Man

Jesus was both fully God and fully human. As a man, he experienced all the physical and emotional limitations of humanity, while being the only person to live a life free from all sin.

● The idea of God becoming man (the Incarnation) is central to Christian beliefs about salvation.

● Only a human could pay the penalty that mankind's sin deserved.

● God could accept only a perfect sacrifice.

● Christians see the death of Jesus on the cross as God's love for humanity and his need for justice coming together in a perfect sacrifice.

● The title Son of Man was used by Jesus of himself.

The Miracles of Jesus

Healing Miracles

There are many stories of Jesus's compassion for those who were suffering, and of dramatic healings. These were not just for effect. They are referred to as signs of the Kingdom of God, examples of the salvation Jesus came to bring. They show his power over all kinds of physical and mental illness.

e.g. He gave new life: Jairus's Daughter (Mark 5,22-42), the Centurion's Servant (Luke 7,1-10).

He gave healthy minds: A mad man in the Synagogue (Mark 1,23-26), a mad man at Gerasa (Mark 5,1-15). He gave healthy bodies: The Paralysed Man (Mark 2,3-12), a leper (Mark 1,40-42), a blind beggar (Mark 10,46-52).

Nature Miracles

The nature miracles are perhaps the hardest to understand. They show that Jesus seemed to have power over nature and could do things which to us appear impossible. The best known of these miracles is the Feeding of the Five Thousand (Mark 6,35-44). Other examples are Jesus's calming of a storm (Mark 4,37-41); changing water into wine (John 2,1-14); causing the great catch of fishes (Luke 5,1-10); and walking on the water (Mark 6,48-51).

The Resurrection

The greatest of all the biblical miracles is the Resurrection, when Jesus rose from the dead on the third day.

- Miracles testify to God's love for suffering humanity.
- The miracles were done in order to lead people to faith in the saving power of God.

The Teaching of Jesus

Jesus's teaching was usually in simple form, with examples from everyday life. It was often very critical of the religious establishment. Most Christians say that Jesus's teaching makes sense only when you know about his death and resurrection. Its basis is: 'Love God and your neighbour as yourself'.

Parables and the Kingdom of God

A parable is a story with two meanings – an obvious, outward 'earthly' meaning and a deeper, underlying 'heavenly' meaning.

A lot of Jesus's teaching was about the Kingdom of God. By this, Jesus meant God's spiritual reign over the world and the people he has made. The people to whom Jesus preached said they could see no sign of this kingdom, so Jesus taught in parables to show what he meant.

In the parable of the *Mustard Seed* (Mark 4,30-32), Jesus taught that God's Kingdom would grow from small beginnings. Similarly, in the *Seed Growing Secretly* (Mark 4,26-29), he taught that the Kingdom will come through God's power.

Other parables teach about God and people:

The Wheat and the Weeds (Matthew 13,24-30). God knows what people are really like, and will one day separate good from bad.

The Sower (Mark 4,3-8). People are different and will respond to God's words in different ways.

The Prodigal Son (Luke 15,11-32), *The Lost Sheep* (Matthew 18,12-13). God cares about people and forgives the repentant sinner.

The Good Samaritan (Luke 10,30-37). People should care for one another.

The Holy Spirit

The early Christians believed that the Holy Spirit, the power of God, was sent from God after the ascension of Jesus.

Christians believe the Spirit to be eternal like Jesus and God. In John's Gospel (14,16), Jesus promises his disciples that God will send '. . . another Counsellor to be with you for ever – the Spirit of truth'. The word 'counsellor' means 'one called alongside to help'. Christians believe that the Holy Spirit helps to make Jesus real and active to his followers today.

Some Christians say that they are 'baptised' of the Spirit, and experience God's love and power in receiving spiritual gifts, such as healing and speaking in tongues. This gives them a new freedom in worshipping him.

• Christians believe that the Holy Spirit:

1. takes ordinary people with all their failings and gradually changes them into the sort of person God wants them to be, so they live better lives;

2. helps people to pray;

3. may guide people in choices and decisions. They believe that the Spirit is God's way of communicating with his people, and may say 'I feel I was led by the Spirit to do . . .'

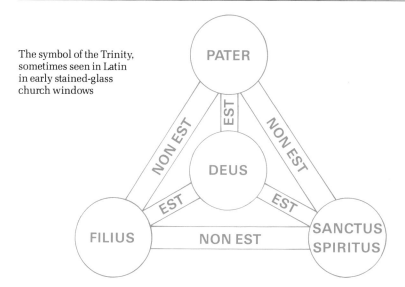

The symbol of the Trinity, sometimes seen in Latin in early stained-glass church windows

The Trinity

Christians believe in one God, but they believe that God has shown himself in three persons – the Father, the Son and the Holy Spirit. They call this the Trinity: always the same God, yet three in one.

- **Father** God is the Creator, source of all things.
- **Son** Jesus is the 'Light' of the World.
- **Holy Spirit** The power of God active in the world, today.
- The Trinity describes God in three relationships to people.

Life after Death

Christians believe that there is life after death. They believe that people retain their identity and individuality after death, but that they will have spiritual bodies. Christian funeral services stress the hope that in time the dead person will be resurrected and reunited with God.

The word 'sleep' is often used for death in the New Testament.

There is also the idea of a point in time known as the Day of Judgement, when all people will be resurrected, judged by God, and enter either hell or heaven.

Hell and Heaven

God's judgement on people's response to Jesus is final and eternal. The punishment for sinners is hell, eternal separation from God. Jesus gave several pictures of hell, including 'deepest darkness', a 'fire that never goes out', and a place of continual decay. It is not a physical place, but is the feeling of utter loneliness and meaninglessness which comes from life without God.

Heaven is also not a physical place, though early Christians, having no modern scientific knowledge of space, thought of it as being beyond the sky. Modern Christians believe that Heaven is the state of life with Christ and, of course, with God, and of being in God's presence for eternity.

- The teaching of Jesus did not concentrate on hell-fire.
- Christians believe that God did not send his Son into the world to condemn the world, but to save the world through him (John 3,17).

Eternal Life

When Jesus promised his followers eternal life, he did not just mean a life with God in heaven. He taught that eternal life starts when a person gives himself or herself over to God's rule. It reaches its fullness after death.

In Christian belief, God's original plan was for humanity to enjoy eternal life in a close relationship with Him. Sin and disobedience cause spiritual death. Becoming a Christian is to rediscover God's original plan and to experience spiritual rebirth, and so return to this close relationship with God.

Christians also believe that eternal life cannot be earned by trying to please God through good deeds. It must be received as a gift resulting from Jesus's sacrifice on the cross.

- Eternal life begins with spiritual rebirth.

2 The Church

The Church as a Body of People

Strictly speaking, the Church is not a building but a fellowship of people. The name comes from a Greek word meaning an assembly, a believing community.

In the letters of the Apostle Paul (e.g. Romans 12,4 and 5), the Church is called *One Body in Christ*. By this, Paul meant that the Church is a unity like the human body; that it is, or should be, one group of people acting together to spread the gospel. The New Testament is quite clear that one of the gravest sins is to destroy the unity of what should be the united body of the Church. This idea is further reinforced by the Apostles' Creed in the statement 'I believe in the *Communion of Saints*' – that is to say, in the caring co-operative 'loving one another' of all those who may be called Christians. (The word 'Saints' here means the members of the Church.)

● The Church as an organised group of people can be said to have its real beginning on the Feast of Pentecost (Acts 2).

● The Church is the instrument and the agent through which people meet Christ.

● The Church is Christ's dwelling-place.

History of the Church

There are three principal divisions of Christianity: Orthodox, Roman Catholic and Protestant. The diagram on page 16 will remind you how these came about.

Each of the three main groupings has suffered persecution over the centuries – sometimes from each other. Differences of opinion within the main traditions have also produced many smaller groups. These groups are known as *denominations*.

The Orthodox Church, for instance, divided into two during the eighth century, for theological reasons. The Church of England, itself a sixteenth-century breakaway from the Roman Catholic Church, subdivided further into Anglicans and those desiring more freedom – the Non-Conformist or Free Churches. More recently, the twentieth century has seen the rapid growth of Pentecostal movements which aim for a return to primitive Christianity.

The main Christian traditions

Jesus

12 Disciples
soon became
5000 Christians

SPREAD OF CHRISTIANITY
The Acts of the Apostles tells of the rapid
spread of Christianity. By AD 60, Paul's missionary
activities take Jesus's message to many parts of the
Roman Empire. Christianity becomes the state
religion of the Empire in the fourth century AD
after the conversion of the Emperor Constantine.

CHRISTIANITY

**EAST-WEST SCHISM
(THE GREAT SCHISM)**
AD 800-1054
Disputes over control of the
Church and differences of ritual
cause a division into an Eastern
church under Constantinople
and a Western church under
Rome.

THE REFORMATION
AD 1500-1600
Attempts to reform the
Roman Catholic Church lead to
a further breakaway.
Protestors inspired by Martin
Luther and John Calvin wish to
follow the teachings found in the
Bible, not those dictated by
human leaders. They establish the
Protestant Churches.

ROMAN CATHOLICISM

PROTESTANT CHRISTIANITY

ECUMENICAL MOVEMENT
AD 1800 – PRESENT
Attempts begin to
reunite the Churches.

ORTHODOX CHRISTIANITY

1000 million
in 1990s

150 million
in 1990s

330 million
in 1990s

Christian Groups

The Orthodox, Roman Catholic and Anglican traditions say that the authority for their leaders can be traced back to Jesus choosing twelve men to be his special disciples. He sent these same men out to do his work and they became Apostles (sent out). He gave them authority to forgive sins. He gave them bread and wine during the last meal he shared with them and told them to 'Do this in remembrance of me' (Luke 22,19).

The twelve became the first leaders of the church. They appointed others to succeed them, called *presbyters* or *bishops*. This succession has been symbolically handed on ever since through the bishops' 'laying-on of hands', an action mentioned several times in the New Testament when early Christians were being given special tasks. It was linked with the receiving of the Spirit and the sharing of the power of God. The 'laying-on of hands' still symbolises that God's work is going on through the Spirit.

The main Christian denominations

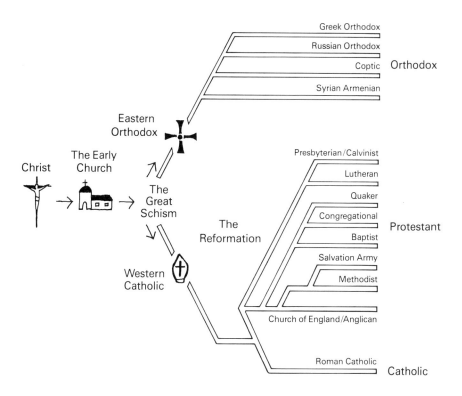

Orthodox Churches

The Orthodox Church is the common name for a group of independent churches, each with its own head, called a Patriarch, which is spread throughout the eastern part of Europe – from Moscow in the north, down to Alexandria, on the northern shore of Africa, in the south. Orthodox Christians have also established communities in other parts of the world, such as Britain, the USA and Australia. The name of the country they came from is usually added to the word Orthodox: for example, Greek Orthodox, Russian Orthodox, etc.

The interiors of Orthodox church buildings are richly decorated with traditional religious pictures, known as *icons*, often depicting Mary the Mother of Jesus, Jesus, and the Apostles. Jesus is emphasised as Victor and King, restoring people to the image of God as described in Genesis. Orthodox Christians recognise seven sacraments.

Leadership of the Orthodox Church

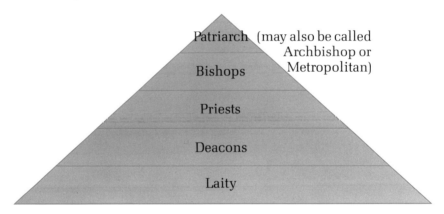

There is no overall leader. Orthodox Churches are divided into Councils called Patriarchies or Metropolitans which are independent of each other. In some areas Bishops are elected; in others they are appointed.

- Liturgy is the essence of Orthodoxy (see Chapter 5).
- The Orthodox Church is unusual for its veneration of icons.
- There are no women clergy.

Roman Catholic Churches

Roman Catholics believe they can trace authority back to Jesus, who told Peter 'Upon you I will found my church'. Peter was the first Bishop of Rome, or Pope. The Bishops of Rome claim a direct link with the Apostles: they see their authority as having been handed on literally from one to the next until the present day.

Roman Catholic thinking stresses the need for good works together with salvation obtained through Jesus. The service of the Mass or Eucharist (bread and wine) is very important, and many pious customs and practices are used as aids in religious life. Roman Catholics also observe seven sacraments.

Leadership of the Catholic Church

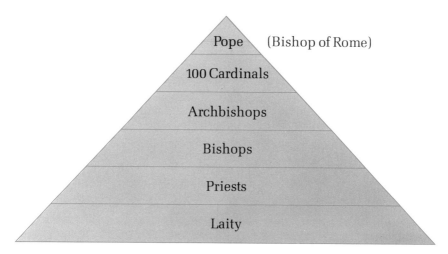

Pope (Bishop of Rome)

100 Cardinals

Archbishops

Bishops

Priests

Laity

The main administrative centre of the Roman Catholic Church is in the Pope's Palace, the Vatican in Rome. The Pope is supported by a college of Cardinals from all over the world. The Church is also divided into dioceses and parishes.

● The Pope speaks for the whole Church in matters of faith and morals.

● Tradition is recorded in scripture and is expressed in church councils.

● There are no women clergy.

Anglican Churches

The Anglican Church has branches in many countries of the world. In England, the Anglican Church is known as the 'Church of England'. In other countries, a title such as the 'Anglican Church of South Africa' may be used. The churches are all said to be part of the Anglican Communion.

The Anglican Church was established in England at the time of Henry VIII. There is a breadth of custom within the Anglican Communion, ranging from those still influenced by the Roman Catholic tradition to those influenced by the Protestant, Non-Conformist tradition.

Leadership of the Church of England

(The Queen)

Archbishops of
Canterbury and York

Bishops

Archdeacons

Rural Deans

Priests, Vicars or Rectors
in charge of parishes

Curates

Deacons/Deaconesses

Laity

The Sovereign must always be a member of the Church of England and upholds it. The Archbishops, Bishops and Deans are appointed by the Sovereign on the advice of the Prime Minister, who considers names submitted by the Church's leadership. All clergy take an oath of allegiance to the Crown.

The Archbishop of Canterbury is 'Primate of All England' and presides over 30 dioceses. The Archbishop of York, 'Primate of England', supervises 14 dioceses. The two Archbishops, the Bishops of London, Durham and Winchester, and the 21 most senior other bishops, sit in the House of Lords.

The central governing body is the General Synod, made up of Archbishops, Bishops, clergy and lay members. The 13 250 parishes are served by the parish priests. The Anglican Church in England does not yet ordain women priests, but women may become deaconesses. A deacon or deaconess may help with caring for the laity and assist at services, but cannot hear confessions or celebrate Holy Communion.

● The Apostles' Creed is the basic statement of belief.
● The possibility of women priests is currently much discussed. In 1987 the General Synod agreed in principle to ordain women priests at some time in the future.

Congregational Churches

Congregationalists reject the idea of a priesthood set apart to lead worship or intercede with God on behalf of the community. They believe in the common priesthood of all members of their congregation. Each local Congregational group organises itself but is expected to share mutual care and concern with other Congregationalists.

Baptist Churches

The Baptist movement developed out of early Congregationalists because the Baptists opposed infant baptism, taking the view that baptism should be reserved for believers old enough to make their own declaration of faith. They also thought that baptism should be done by dipping completely under water, not merely by being sprinkled with water.

Baptists accept the authority of the Bible as their guide to faith. They practise believer's baptism and limit membership to believers only. Like the Congregationalists, they think all members are capable of serving as priests, and ministers are elected by their congregation. Each Baptist church runs its own affairs, though a group of churches may form a regional association for exchange of views.

Presbyterian Churches

Presbyterians have a simple and orderly worship stressing the word of God. Their beliefs are based on John Calvin's teaching, and they look to the New Testament idea of a group of leaders called *elders* to lead and direct God's people.

United Reformed Church

In 1972 the Congregationalist and Presbyterian Churches in England forged an Act of Union combining themselves into one body – the United Reformed Church. Some groups, however, preferred to remain separate, so Congregational and Presbyterian churches still exist.

The United Reformed Church is run by a General Assembly, made up of twelve provinces called synods. Each province has a moderator who acts as an overseer. There are seventy District Councils. Men and women clergy, called ministers, are elected by each individual congregation.

The Religious Society of Friends (Quakers)

The Society of Friends was formed in the seventeenth century by George Fox, a Puritan and the son of a weaver. His main belief was that people could feel direct spiritual experiences from God. Meetings are essentially silent, with any member free to speak as the Spirit leads.

Members of the Society of Friends soon got the nickname 'Quakers' because they were said to quake or tremble under the influence of the Spirit. Quakers respect everybody because they believe there is a 'divine light' in each person.

● Quakers consider all people to be equal, and in the past have refused special titles which would give them higher positions in society.

● For the same reason, Quakers do not have leaders of their groups.

● They refuse to take oaths (such as promising to tell the truth) because they say a person's word should be enough.

● They are invariably pacifists and refuse to fight in wartime because they say it is unlawful to kill another person.

The Methodist Church

Methodism grew from the preaching of John Wesley, although he always insisted that he was, and would die, a member of the Church of England. While living in London, Wesley preached wherever he was invited, but his invitations were few because his message was uncomfortable. He began preaching in the open air and travelled to many towns in England. John Wesley was assisted in his preaching by his brother Charles, who wrote many beautiful hymns.

Wesley always encouraged people to attend Anglican churches, and early Methodists were mainly Anglicans who gathered into 'societies' and accepted the guidance of John Wesley. Eventually, after Wesley's death, the societies left the Church of England and formed the Wesleyan Methodist Church.

Other Methodist societies, e.g. the Primitive Methodists and the United Methodists, along with the Wesleyan Methodists, all reunited in 1922 to form the Methodist Church. However, the Independent Methodists and the Wesleyan Reform Union still exist as separate branches of Methodism.

Methodist clergy are called ministers and may be men or women. The Methodist Church is governed by the Methodist Conference, which is divided into 34 districts and then into 900 circuits under superintendent ministers. People from the laity help with the preaching and are called lay preachers.

- Methodists have a strong musical tradition in the hymns of Charles Wesley and others.
- Church organisation is thought less important than that 'the church should be God's missionary force in the world'.
- Early Methodists were particularly notable for reaching the poor.

The Salvation Army

The Salvation Army developed from the Methodist Church. William Booth was a Methodist minister who left the Church in 1861 in order to work in the East End slums. His early converts were the poor and uneducated who were intimidated by formal church worship. Booth therefore established mission stations so that converts would have somewhere informal to assemble and worship.

At first, the work was organised under the name of the Christian Mission. Later, the name Salvation Army was adopted and the organisation was set up along military lines. Leaders hold military-style ranks, with a general in overall command, supported by majors, captains and lieutenants. It is one of the Salvation Army's great principles that women have absolute equality with men.

Pentecostalism

Pentecostalism has become a force within Christianity during the twentieth century. Pentecostalist thinking is based on the importance of the first Pentecost and the belief that all Christians must experience a similar spiritual awakening during their lives. Pentecostalists speak of this as the Baptism of the Spirit. They stress commitment and evangelisation, together with a strict moral code based on the Bible. There is also a strong belief in *charism* which is a gift from God to an individual, e.g. the charism of preaching or the speaking in tongues. Worship is lively, often loud, and usually informal. The churches act independently, but may be part of a federation such as the Church of God of Prophecy or the Assemblies of God.

The Renewal Movement

There is a Renewal Movement in most of the established churches. This is a re-awakening to Pentecostal values by practising members of the faith. While remaining within their own Christian tradition, they respond to a Pentecostal experience.

The House Church Movement

This is one of the newest and most rapidly growing movements. As the title suggests, worship and meetings are usually held in homes, and are very informal. The House Church Movement consider that they are re-establishing the form of worship used by the early Christians and established by Christ. A House Church group may be part of a denominational church or may have no direct link.

In these churches, all members share all responsibilities. An elder may be elected to run the church.

World Council of Churches (WCC)

The World Council of Churches works to bring Christian denominations closer together. Over 300 denominations are now members. Roman Catholic and some Pentecostalist churches have not joined. The WCC work includes:

- working for Christian unity by studying and discussing beliefs and practices which have caused divisions in the Church;
- working together in missionary activities at home and abroad;
- working for justice in the world;
- providing help in developing countries and other areas where there is racial inequality or oppression;
- helping local Christian groups.

The Council of Churches for Britain and Ireland (CCBI)

The Council of Churches for Britain and Ireland is linked to the World Council of Churches and does similar work. The best known of its activities is Christian Aid week, held every year to raise money throughout the UK for the work of helping the poor and needy.

3 | The Bible

The Bible is a library of sixty-six books. Some of these are among the oldest literature in the world. There are two large sections, the *Old Testament* and the *New Testament*, and a smaller one known as the *Apocrypha*, which is usually only found in Bibles used by Roman Catholics.

The word *testament* means 'agreement'. The Old Testament tells of God's agreement with His chosen people, the Jews, to bring them a messiah in return for them worshipping God alone; for Christians, the New Testament records God's fulfilment of that agreement.

The Old Testament

The Pentateuch

Genesis
Exodus
Leviticus
Numbers
Deuteronomy

The word Pentateuch means 'the first five books'. Traditionally they are said to have been written by Moses.

Genesis, the first book of the Bible, deals with:

1. the creation of the universe and the origin of humankind;

2. humankind's relationship to God;

3. how human pride spoiled the relationship, the fall into sin, and the judgement which followed;

4. the beginning of the story of the early Israelites, a people chosen by God to carry his message to the whole human race, the promise made to Abraham by God and the *covenant* (agreement) made through him to all the Jews.

While Genesis tells stories about people, it is mainly an account of what God did. Throughout, the main influence is God who shapes history.

Exodus tells how the 'chosen people' became slaves in Egypt, and how Moses, the man sent by God, led them to freedom and told them God's laws. Above all, this book tells how God liberated his people and formed them into a nation with hope for the future.

Leviticus, Numbers and *Deuteronomy* give more details of the laws that Jews must live by in obedience to God.

History

Joshua
Judges
Ruth
1 & 2 Samuel
1 & 2 Kings
1 & 2 Chronicles
Ezra
Nehemiah
Esther

Joshua and *Judges* tell the history of how the Jews invaded and settled in the 'promised land', Canaan.

Ruth, Samuel, Kings, Chronicles, Ezra, Nehemiah and *Esther* continue the history of Israel up to the Exile in Babylon.

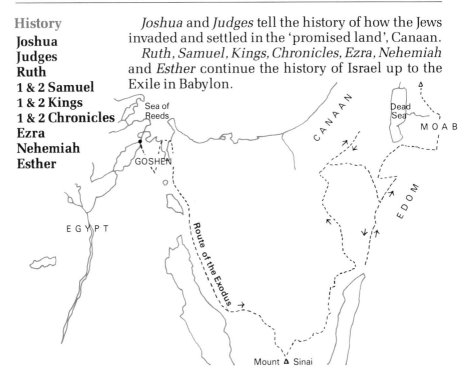

Poetry and Wisdom

Job
Psalms
Proverbs
Ecclesiastes
Song of Solomon

The book of *Job* tells of the problems of suffering, and how suffering is not caused by sin.

The book of *Psalms* contains 150 hymns which are used in worship by both Jews and Christians. There are five groups of *Psalms*:

● hymns of praise and worship of God;
● prayers for help, protection and salvation;
● pleas for forgiveness;
● songs of thanksgiving for God's blessings;
● petitions for the punishment of enemies.

The book of *Proverbs* is a collection of wise sayings and advice on how to live as God requires.

In the book of *Ecclesiastes*, people are urged by 'the Philosopher' to work hard and to enjoy the gifts of God.

The *Song of Solomon* or *Song of Songs* is a collection of love poems. The songs have been interpreted by Jews as a picture of the relationship between God and humanity, and by Christians as a picture of the relationship between Christ and the Church.

The Prophets

Isaiah
Jeremiah
Lamentations
Ezekiel
Daniel
Hosea
Joel
Amos
Obadiah
Jonah
Micah
Nahum
Habakkuk
Zephaniah
Haggai
Zechariah
Malachi

The books named after *Prophets* trace more of the history of the Jews to the end of the Old Testament. These books show that many Jews did not feel the need of God's laws. They were unfaithful to him and so a new agreement was needed between God and man. The prophets brought this new message and warned what would happen if God's message was ignored.

The book of *Lamentations* is a collection of five poems lamenting the destruction of Jerusalem by the Babylonians and the aftermath of ruin and exile, but there is a note of trust in God and hope for the future.

The Apocrypha (Deuterocanonical Books)

Tobit
Judith
Wisdom
Ecclesiasticus
Baruch
1 & 2 Maccabees

The Apocrypha forms a bridge between the Old and New Testaments. Like the Old Testament, its contents are a mixture of history, religious fiction, and Wisdom literature.

The word *apocrypha* means 'hidden writings'.

The books of the Apocrypha are thought by Protestants to lack the divine inspiration of the rest of the Bible, so they tend not to appear in Protestant Bibles. In Roman Catholic Bibles they are known as the Deuterocanonical Books.

The New Testament

The New Testament sets out to show that Jesus is the Messiah, the saviour foretold in the Old Testament. The themes of the New Testament are Jesus, and his relationship with God and with people. It sets out a new agreement between God and all people, with Jesus as the key to this new agreement.

At first, the stories of the life and teaching of Jesus were handed down by word of mouth. Eventually, they were collected together in four books known as Gospels: Matthew, Mark, Luke and John. Gospel means 'good news'. The good news of Jesus's message was that he was the promised Messiah, the Son of God, sent to save everyone.

Each Gospel presents the life and work of Jesus in a different way. The first three (Matthew, Mark and Luke) are called the Synoptic Gospels because they describe events from the same point of view and have a lot in common.

Jesus and the early Church

Matthew

Mark

Luke

John

Acts of the Apostles

Matthew, a Jew, wanted to show how the life of Jesus fulfilled the prophecies about the Messiah in Jewish scripture. This Gospel presents Jesus as the great Teacher, who teaches about God's kingdom.

Mark wrote mainly for Christians who were being persecuted in Rome. He probably got much of his information from the Apostle Peter. Jesus is pictured as a man of action and authority, speaking of himself as the Son of Man, who came to give his life to set people free from sin.

Luke, a Gentile doctor, who also wrote the book of Acts of the Apostles, and was a friend and companion of the Apostle Paul, missionary to the Gentiles, recorded the life of Jesus to back up Paul's teaching. Luke showed that Jesus loved outcasts and sinners, and that he had a high respect for women, which was unusual in those days. This Gospel presents Jesus as the Saviour of all humankind with a concern for people with all kinds of needs

John wrote his Gospel last, probably about AD 90. He stresses from the start that Jesus was divine and concentrates on Jesus teaching his disciples. This Gospel is written so that readers will believe that Jesus is the promised saviour, the Son of God, and that through faith in Jesus all may have eternal life.

The *Acts of the Apostles* is a continuation of the Gospel of Luke and describes the growth of the Christian church as the followers of Jesus spread his message and established early churches in many parts of the Roman Empire. Acts tells also of the dramatic conversion of Saul, who had been a persecutor of the first Christians until he received a vision of Jesus that made him convert to Christianity. After his conversion, Saul was known by the name Paul. The rest of Acts is largely concerned with the work Paul did to convert thousands of people to belief in Jesus. After describing Paul's doings on his three missionary journeys, the book ends with an account of his arrest and imprisonment in Jerusalem and of his eventful journey by way of Malta to Rome.

Epistles

Romans
1 & 2 Corinthians
Galatians
Ephesians
Philippians
Colossians
1 & 2
Thessalonians
1 & 2 Timothy
Titus
Philemon
Hebrews
James
1 & 2 Peter
1, 2 & 3 John
Jude

The *Epistles* are letters written mostly by Paul to the early churches. Some were written to individual Christians. All were written to help Christians to understand how to behave according to the message of Jesus.

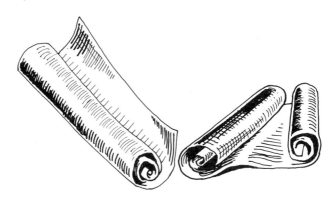

Revelation

The *Book of Revelation* contains visions of God's supremacy and his final triumph over evil at the end of time, the Apocalypse. It is written in picture language with hidden meanings that are sometimes hard to understand. Christians believe the hidden meaning is 'Be patient, times may be grim, but God will save those who trust him.'

● The Bible is the basis of belief and teaching for the whole Christian Church.

● The *canonical* writings are those accepted by Christians as divinely inspired – the Old and New Testaments.

● The *Deuterocanonical Books* are not usually accorded the same status by Protestants as the Old and New Testaments, though there is much in them of value.

● The Gospels are four different portraits of Jesus. They have a great deal in common.

● The writers of the Gospels are known as *evangelists.*

How the Bible Reached its Present Form

Most of the books in the Old Testament were handed down by word of mouth for centuries before being written down. The earliest known copies were written on scrolls of papyrus. Some of these were found near the Dead Sea in 1947 and are known as the Dead Sea Scrolls. Later copies were written in *codex* (book) form.

By the time of Jesus all the books in the Old Testament were known, written down and used by the Jews. The collection was finally accepted by the Jewish Synod at Jamnia in AD 90. The first Christians continued to use the Jewish scriptures.

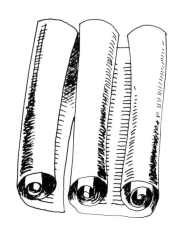

The first New Testament documents to be written down were the Epistles written by Paul. These were read and reread by the people they had been written for, and were copied and sent to other Christians to be read aloud when Christians met together. The four Gospels were also written down during the first century, probably on papyrus.

The last book in the Bible, Revelation, was written about AD 96. These 27 books were used for many years and in AD 367 they were formally accepted by a group of church leaders and became known as the *Canon of the New Testament*, the books which contained the true teaching of the Church.

There are many famous copies of parts of the Bible, all in codex form:

1. The Codex Sinaiticus is named after the monastery on Mount Sinai where it was found. It contains the whole of the New Testament and parts of the Old Testament.

2. The Codex Alexandrinus is named after Alexandria in Egypt where it was found.

3. The Codex Vaticanus is kept in the Vatican in Rome, as the name suggests.

Versions of the Bible

The Old Testament was originally written in Hebrew, although by the time Jesus was alive it had been translated into Greek. The Greek translation was used mainly by Jews who lived outside Palestine. It was known as the *Septuagint*. Jesus would have used the Hebrew version.

The New Testament was written mainly in Greek, but partly in Aramaic. Greek was the common language in that part of the world at the time of Jesus.

The Bible was next translated into Latin, the official language of the Roman Empire. Soon there were many different versions and so Pope Damasus ordered his secretary Jerome to make a new one that became known as the *Vulgate* (meaning 'common' or 'popular'). This version was used for centuries in Europe, even though Latin was not spoken by ordinary people. Demand grew for mother-tongue Bibles.

In England, Church leaders, nobles and kings were against the Bible being translated into English; but translators such as John Wycliffe and William Tyndale risked their lives to make copies available to literate people. Times changed. Soon after he came to the throne, James I ordered a group of scholars to produce a new translation of the Bible. This was published in 1611 and became known as the *Authorised Version*, or King James Bible. This version was used in churches in England until the 1960s and remains the best-known English language version of the Bible.

A revision of the Authorised Version, the *Revised Standard Version*, was published in 1952 in the light of increased knowledge of the original Hebrew and Greek texts. The New Testament of the New English Bible, a new translation, was introduced in 1961, to be followed by the Old Testament in 1970. This was followed by the *Good News Bible*, a modern translation in straightforward, non-academic English. The *Jerusalem Bible*, a version approved by the Roman Catholic Church, appeared at about the same time: it has difficult sections but is considered very good for reading aloud.

The *New International Version* (1979) is an attempt to produce a dignified version in the tradition of earlier English Bibles. This is the Bible used for quotations in most examination syllabuses.

The Authority of the Bible

Christians regard the Bible as divinely inspired. It is their holy book. But though all Christians agree that the Bible is 'the word of God', they hold varying views on what this means.

'Word by Word' View – Fundamentalist/Literalist Approach

Some Christians believe that every word in the Bible was directly inspired by God: that He guided the thought of the authors of the books to write exactly what He wanted to say. They believe that every word is the literal truth. Such Christians are known as *fundamentalists.*

'Stage by Stage' View – a Conservative Approach

Other Christians believe that, through the Bible, God has gradually revealed Himself and His wishes for people. Through the Bible, Christians are steadily shown the nature of God. The stories teach that

God is a god of justice and love, a creator who cares for the unfortunate and who promised and sent a saviour, deliverer for all people.

'All About Jesus' View

Some believe that the really special thing about the Bible is that it explains everything about Jesus.

- The Old Testament prepares the way for Jesus.
- The Old Testament contains many predictions that God will send a Saviour/Messiah and these are predictions about the coming of Jesus.
- The Gospels in the New Testament show that these predictions had come true, and also give the message of Jesus for the whole world.
- The Acts of the Apostles and the Epistles show how this message was spread in the world.
- The Book of Revelation includes a vision of heaven to which Jesus ascended.

'Main Ideas' View

Some Christians believe that God speaks to them through the main ideas found in the Bible. Certain parts of the Bible are thus more important than others. Main ideas include the following:

- There is only one God, who created everything.
- People must obey God.
- Jesus shows people most clearly what God is like.
- God cares for all, His love does not depend on race, colour, sex, health and strength, wealth or intelligence.
- Jesus taught people how to live as God wishes.
- Those who are sorry for their sins turn to God for forgiveness, follow Jesus, and can inherit life after death.

4 Christian Values

Christians share a set of values which are an important part of their faith and which can affect every part of their lives.

The Image of God

The story of creation in Genesis shows humans to be the most important part of God's creation. This creation was originally without fault, without evil and without death. Humans are described as being made 'in the image of God' (Genesis 1,27), with a special place in the order of things. They can choose either to obey God or to disobey Him. The story of Adam and Eve choosing to disobey and become independent of God is known as *The Fall*. Christians believe it was as a result of this disobedience that evil and sin came into the world.

Genesis also says: 'God blessed them (humans) and said to them "Be fruitful and increase in number; fill the earth and subdue it." ' (1,28). It is how Christians interpret this passage which affects their attitudes towards abortion, birth control, euthanasia, conservation, pollution. They may ask themselves, 'What are we doing to God's creation?'.

Personal Conduct

Basic Rules for Living (Mark 12,28-31)

Jesus reminded his listeners that God wanted people to live in a certain way, according to certain values – not just to go to the Temple and synagogue, and perform rituals at home. Jesus respected and reinforced Old Testament moral laws. He taught that the most important commandments were as follows:

'Hear, O Israel, the Lord our God is one. Love the Lord your God with all your heart and with all your soul and with all your mind and with all your strength . . . .

Love your neighbour as yourself.

There is no commandment greater than these.'

Love (1 Corinthians 13)

Love is the most important standard used in the New Testament. In his letter to the Corinthians, the Apostle Paul says that the best actions, including gifts to charity and even martyrdom, are worthless without love: he makes it clear that love should be part of the character of Christians.

Christan love or *agapé* (pronounced aga-pay) means:

- caring for those who seem unattractive or unlovable;
- wanting the best for those who are not friendly towards you, even loving one's enemies;
- meeting the needs of anyone who is poor or in any kind of need.

Sacrifice (John 15,13)

Most Christians believe that the real meaning of love can be seen in how Jesus was willing to sacrifice everything, even his own life, for his followers: 'Greater love has no one than this, that he lay down his life for his friends.' Christians who have followed this example and died for their beliefs are known as *martyrs*.

The Sermon on the Mount (Matthew 5-7)

The Sermon on the Mount is a guide to the right way of living in the Kingdom of Heaven, as Matthew calls the Kingdom of God. The Sermon on the Mount contains much basic Christian teaching.

The Sermon starts (5,3-12) with the *Beatitudes*. (The word *beatitude* means 'happiness' or 'blessedness'.) The Beatitudes reverse the values of the world, emphasising that true happiness comes from dependence upon God and His will, rather than from self-assertion.

'Blessed are the poor in spirit, for theirs is the kingdom of heaven.

Blessed are those who mourn, for they will be comforted.

Blessed are the meek, for they will inherit the earth.

Blessed are those who hunger and thirst for righteousness, for they shall be filled.

Blessed are the merciful, for they will be shown mercy.

Blessed are the pure in heart, for they will see God.

Blessed are the peacemakers, for they will be called sons of God.

Blessed are those who are persecuted because of righteousness, for theirs is the kingdom of heaven.'

Jesus then gives positive teaching about topics dealt with in the Jewish law, including anger, adultery, divorce, revenge and vows.

Love. The Old Law said 'Love your friends, hate your enemies'; Jesus says 'Love your enemies' (5,25).

Charity. There is a right way to give to the less well-off (6,1-4). It must be done quietly and privately, not for glory among men but for the glory of God. God sees and knows.

Prayer. Prayers should be made in private to God (6,5-13). Jesus gives a model prayer, the *Lord's Prayer*, which deals with the glory of God and the needs of mankind.

Fasting. Followers are not to make a great show when they fast (6,16-18). Jesus pointed out that God, himself unseen, will know they are fasting.

Judgement. Jesus makes it clear that his followers must forgive others and be forgiven by God (7,1-5). They must not judge others. God is the Judge.

● The Sermon on the Mount turns ordinary ideas of human happiness upside-down.

● It is those who set their sights on what is right, not the ruthless go-getters, who will be truly happy.

Mission (Matthew 28,18-20)

Many Christians think it is vital to tell non-Christians about the Christian way of life. They want to *convert* people to Christianity. This is because they believe that:

● the only way to have a right relationship with God is through belief in Jesus, so everyone should hear this important good news;

● Jesus commissioned all Christians to the good news.

Other Christians think that it is not the job of the church to convert people. Rather, since God's work can be seen wherever people are working for peace and justice and against oppression and inequality, Christians should help with this sort of missionary work.

Service (Matthew 25,31-46)

The parable of the Sheep and the Goats is the last in Matthew's Gospel. It is a Jewish picture of the Son of Man on his royal throne surrounded by all his angels, where he divides the people of all nations as a shepherd divides his sheep and goats. The parable teaches that God judges people simply on how they have reacted to those in need. The deeper meaning is that if we help someone else, we give service to Jesus himself. The pictures of heaven and hell remind us that we destroy ourselves if we lead a totally selfish and heartless way of life.

Old Testament Moral Laws (Exodus 20,1-17)

The Ten Commandments are the oldest record we have of Jewish laws. They are remarkable in that they rest on the authority of God and are the same for all people, regardless of status. The first four Commandments are connected with the need to love God, and the last six with the need for people to love each other:

- You shall have no other gods before me.
- You shall not make idols and worship them.
- You shall not misuse the name of the Lord your God.
- Remember the Sabbath day and keep it holy.
- Honour your father and your mother.
- You shall not murder.
- You shall not commit adultery.
- You shall not steal.
- You shall not give false testimony.
- You shall not covet.

Christians continued to accept these rules as Christianity broke away from Judaism. Today, the Commandments still form the basis of many of the laws and rules for peaceful living in many societies, but everyday behaviour in much of the western world has become increasingly *secular* (non-religious).

5 | Christian Worship

Places of Worship

Churches are built for two reasons:

1. To provide a place for people to worship.
2. As an act of worship – to please God by creating a beautiful building.

The earliest churches were built about AD 300 when the Emperor Constantine made Christianity the official religion of the Roman Empire. These were halls like the ones the Romans used for meetings, but with a semicircular bulge at the east end called an *apse*. The apse faced east so that the rising sun would shine through the window and remind Christians that Jesus rose from the dead, and that Jesus is 'the light of the world'.

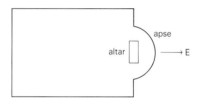

As clergy became more numerous and important, the apse grew bigger until it became a second room used by them in services. The buildings, too, increased in size with the addition of side rooms and small chapels.

Many old churches were built in the shape of a cross. They were divided by a carved screen into two main sections:

the *chancel* where the priest and choir sat;

the *nave* where the people sat (or stood).

The altar was usually the focal point.

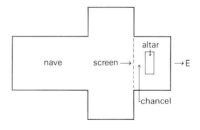

Frequently, parish churches have a tower at the opposite end to the altar. This may be surmounted by a spire reaching upwards to remind Christians of heaven. Tall pointed windows have a similar function.

The churchyard, or land round the church, is considered to be holy ground. Evergreens such as yews, holly and firs are a regular feature among gravestones and war memorials, and remind Christians that Jesus is alive.

Features of a Church of England Parish Church

Many parish churches are something like this plan.

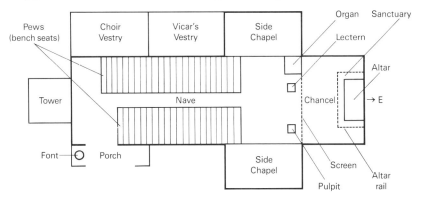

Nave. The large central area is called the nave. For many years there was no seating: the congregation stood or knelt down during the service. Today, there are *pews* to sit on and *hassocks* for people to kneel on when they pray.

Chancel. The chancel is often separated from the nave by an open screen. If the screen has figures of John and the Virgin Mary along with a crucifix on the top, it is known as a *Rood Screen*. ('Rood' is an old word for cross.) The chancel is in two sections:

1. The Choir. The choir is where the clergy and choir sit. It is also where the organ is located.

2. The Sanctuary. This is the most important part of the church, located at the far end of the chancel. The *altar* or Communion-table is here. The design of the church thus concentrates attention on the altar, emphasising the importance of Holy Communion in church life. The altar may be covered with an embroidered or plain white altar-cloth. Candles on the altar remind Christians that Jesus is the 'light of the world'. A cross on the altar recalls the death and resurrection of Jesus. An *altar rail* divides the sanctuary from the choir. Consecrated bread and wine that has been left over from Holy Communion is placed in a wall cupboard known as the *aumbry*. Near the aumbry, a lamp is often kept burning to show that God is always present.

Pulpit. The raised and enclosed platform from which the sermon is preached is usually at the end of the nave near the chancel. Opposite the pulpit there is a stand for the Bible, called the *lectern*.

Font. The font is rather like a basin on a stand. It holds the water used for baptism and is often carved out of stone with a wooden cover over the top. Its location in the nave, near the entrance to the church, is to symbolise that a person starts a new life after baptism.

- The altar is the focal point of a parish church.

Features of an Orthodox Church

An Orthodox church has a *dome* which represents heaven. The building is square to remind worshippers they are equal before God. The floor represents the Earth where all the people gather to stand in front of God.

The main body of the church, the nave, is separated from the sanctuary by an *iconostasis*, a screen covered with icons. Icons are holy paintings of incidents from the life of Jesus, Mary and important saints of the church.

There are three doors in the iconostasis. One leads to the room where the priest puts on his vestments and where the book used for reading the Gospels is kept. Another door leads to the Chapel of Preparation where bread and wine are prepared for the Liturgy. Double doors in the centre, called *Royal Doors*, lead to the holy table called the Holy Throne, on which the bread and wine are blessed to make them holy as the body and blood of Jesus.

Orthodox Christians think of parts of their Liturgy as mysteries which should be hidden from ordinary people. The iconostasis separates them from the sanctuary, just as they are separated from God; and also symbolises that people cannot see God but can get to know him through what he allows them to learn about himself through Jesus and the saints on the icons. The doors symbolise Christ ending the separation between God and people.

Orthodox Christians stand for prayer. There are seats round the walls for the elderly and the sick.

Features of a Roman Catholic Church

Roman Catholic churches show some differences from Church of England parish churches.

The altar, located in the sanctuary, is once again the focal point of the worship; and it is here every day that the priest performs the central act of Roman Catholic worship, the *Mass*.

The Tabernacle. Behind the altar there is a small cupboard or box called the tabernacle, in which some of the consecrated hosts (bread wafers blessed during Mass) are kept. This is the Blessed Sacrament, referred to as the Body of Christ, in which Catholics believe Jesus Christ is truly present. A light near the tabernacle reminds Catholics of Christ's presence.

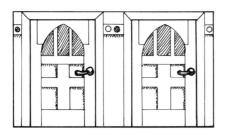

Confession Box. This is a small room or cubicle where a Catholic can, in complete privacy, confess his or her sins to a priest and ask to be forgiven.

Stations of the Cross. Around the walls of the church can be seen fourteen pictures or carvings known as the Stations of the Cross. These show the last journey of Jesus as he carried the cross to his place of crucifixion. They are used especially in the days before Easter to help Catholics in their prayers and thoughts.

Statues. Statues of Jesus, Mary, the disciples and other saints are a familiar feature.

Lady Chapel. There is always a chapel dedicated to the Virgin Mary. It contains her statue and many lighted candles put there by people offering prayers to God.

Candles. Candles are also to be seen on the altar and in many parts of the church. These have been lit to thank God or to ask for His help.

Holy Water. At each entrance, there is a small basin called a *stoop* which contains water. Those entering the church dip their fingers in the stoop and make a sign of the cross on their forehead.

Features of Some Free Churches

Baptist, Methodist, United Reformed, Congregationalist, Presbyterian and other groups use churches (or chapels) different in layout from Catholic or Anglican churches.

The worship area is one large room, often with a rectangular plan. There is a large *pulpit* with a lectern for the Bible. The pulpit is usually a wooden platform with steps leading up to it from both sides. Free Churches believe that the preaching of the word of God is the most important element in worship, so the pulpit is centrally placed. The Communion-table stands in front of the pulpit and is a small, simple wooden table used during Communion. Sometimes, there are no candles and no cross. The organ is often behind the pulpit.

In large Free Churches, a *gallery* runs round three sides of the building. The font is a small basin on a stand near the pulpit or on the Communion-table. Baptists have a large tank (baptistry) for total-immersion baptisms. It is covered when not in use. The building and decorations are in each case much plainer than in parish churches.

- Free Churches have the pulpit as the focal point of the church.

Features of a Quaker Meeting-House

Quakers call their place of worship a Meeting-House. It is plain, with nothing to catch the eye or ear. The meeting-room has benches or seats set in a circle with rows two or three deep. There is a table in the middle with a vase of flowers, a few Bibles and the Quaker book called 'Christian Faith and Practice in the Experience of the Society of Friends'.

Features of a Salvation Army Citadel

The Salvation Army meeting-place is called a Citadel and has little similarity to other churches. At the end of the building there is usually a large platform with chairs, on which sit the band and songsters. Those leading the meeting sit in front of them and behind the speaker's stand – called the *rostrum*. In front of the rostrum is the *mercy seat* where people sit who wish to confess publicly that they have sinned and then ask to be forgiven and so saved. Flags and flowers decorate the building. In front of the platform is the Holiness Table on which is a large open Bible. This serves as a sign that through the words of the Bible, Salvationists are brought closer to God.

Public Acts of Worship

In the Christian Church, a public act of worship takes place when a group of believers, called a *congregation*, come together to praise and thank God, to confess their sorrow for their sins, and to ask Him for help and guidance to live a better life.

Sunday is the day most Christians meet for worship: it is the day Jesus rose from the dead, as well as the day God began His creation.

Liturgical and Non-Liturgical Worship

The word liturgy means 'service to God'. Worship is seen as the best sort of service to God, and the word is often used to describe the different forms or patterns of the Eucharist, Holy Communion or Mass. This applies particularly to the Orthodox, Roman Catholic and Anglican Churches. Liturgical worship follows a set order, usually printed in a prayer book, with set symbolic actions such as processions, standing, sitting and kneeling at different points.

Some of the Protestant churches have developed a *non-liturgical* style which allows people to take a greater part in their services. There is more preaching, more Bible reading and more community hymn-singing. Holy Communion (see below) is celebrated less often. Prayers are made up according to the needs of the day.

Sacramental Services

The most frequent sacramental service is the one based on the Last Supper at which bread and wine are given to the congregation (1 Corinthians 11,23-26). This has a variety of names:

The Lord's Supper. A Biblical title recalling Jesus's last supper with his disciples.

The Eucharist. The Greek word Eucharist means thanksgiving. Jesus gave thanks over the bread and wine. Today Christians give thanks for what God has done for them, and for the life and sacrifice of Jesus.

The Mass. The name used by Roman Catholics. It comes from the concluding dismissory Latin words, 'Ite, missa est.'

Holy Communion. This means the 'common sharing', because everyone is sharing with each other and with Jesus. It is the name used by Anglicans.

The Breaking of Bread. A name given to the service by some Free Churches.

In Roman Catholic and Anglican churches, a cup known as a *chalice* is used to hold the wine. The bread is held on a plate called a *paten* or in a covered vessel called a *ciborium*. This bread may be a special thin, round type called a *wafer*, or it may be ordinary bread, broken or cut up into small pieces. In Free Churches the wine is in individual wine glasses and pieces of ordinary bread are used.

By whatever name it is known, this is a powerfully symbolic service. The following are some of its meanings:

- It is a way of offering oneself to God.
- It is a way of praising and thanking God.
- Many believers feel they are sharing a great closeness with Jesus and with the other Christians who take part in the service.
- Many people believe that the bread stands for the body of Jesus and the wine for his blood; they remember how he died to save them and consider the Eucharist as a form of re-enactment of the sacrifice of Jesus.
- Many feel united with Jesus; they say Jesus is present in the bread and wine and in the people who meet together to remember him.
- Roman Catholics and Orthodox Christians believe that the bread and wine actually become the body and blood of Jesus. This is the doctrine of *transubstantiation*.

The service may also include hymns, prayers, Bible readings, and a sermon.

Non-Sacramental Services

A non-sacramental service is one that does not involve the bread and wine. Forms of non-sacramental worship are held in all Christian Churches. The following order of service is typical of most denominations, except perhaps Quakers:

Hymn. Clergy and choir enter the church.

Prayers. Confessing sins and asking God's forgiveness. Praising God.

Psalms. Sometimes sung, sometimes read; they also praise God.

Bible reading. From Old and New Testaments, different each week.

Creed. Allows Christians to state their beliefs. Only said in Orthodox, Roman Catholic and Anglican churches.

Prayers. Longer prayers asking God to help and guide people.

Hymn.

Sermon. A talk usually based on a text/verse from one of the Bible readings.

Collection of money (during which hymn is sung). Used for upkeep of church as well as charity.

Blessing. Last prayers.

Hymn.

Eucharist in the Orthodox Church

A normal Sunday Eucharist in the Orthodox Church follows 'The Liturgy of St John Chrysostom' who was Patriarch of Constantinople in the fourth century.

The following sequence gives a brief outline:

1. Preparation of the Bread and Wine. This is done by the priest in the Chapel of Preparation, a small room to the left of the icon screen.

2. The Litany of Peace. Litany is an ancient form of prayer which began in the Eastern Church. It consists of a series of petitions or short prayers sung or said by the priest. The choir and people respond by saying 'Kyrie eleison' – 'Lord, have mercy.'

3. The Beatitudes. See page 33.

4. Readings from the Bible. Psalms, Epistles, Gospels.

5. The Great Entrance. A procession, led by the priest or priests, carries the bread and wine in the holy vessels, accompanied by servers with candles and incense. As they pass through the worshippers in the church, the people bow in reverence. The Royal Doors are opened, and the priest goes through and lays the bread and wine on the Holy Throne (the holy table).

6. Kiss of Peace and the Creed. Worshippers greet one another with the Kiss of Peace, and everyone recites the Nicene Creed.

7. Prayers of the Eucharist. Thanksgiving, ending with the Gospel story of the Last Supper. Remembrance, calling to mind Christ's death and resurrection. Consecration of the holy gifts. The Lord's Prayer.

8. Elevation and Fraction. The priest raises the consecrated bread for all to see and then breaks it into small pieces. The choir sings, and the bells are rung.

9. Communion of Priests and People. The priest comes and stands in front of the Royal Doors and those who are taking communion come forward to receive a piece of the holy bread dipped in wine and served on a spoon.

10. The Antidoron. Everyone present comes up to kiss the cross which the priest holds, and to receive a small piece of bread, called the antidoron. It is shared as a sign of fellowship and love, like the meals the early Christians used to share together.

Mass in the Roman Catholic Church

An account of the way in which the mass is celebrated in the Roman Catholic church is given in Chapter 19.

Holy Communion in the Church of England

The following sequence gives a brief outline.

The service is in two parts:

The Word of God (1-5);

The Sacrament (6-10).

1. Preparation. Prayers including the 'Kyrie eleison' and the 'Gloria'. Confession.

2. Bible Readings. From the Old Testament, the Epistles and the Gospels.

3. Sermon. Usually based on a text from the readings.

4. The Creed. All stand to recite the Nicene Creed.

5. Prayers. Of Intercession (for the whole Christian Church and the world). Of Humble Access (thanking God for all he has done).

6. The Peace. The congregation may greet each other by shaking hands as a symbol that they wish each other peace.

7. The Offertory. Bread and wine are taken to the altar. Money is collected. The money is used for the upkeep of the Church and for charity. People offer money and themselves to God.

8. The Eucharistic Prayer. Spoken by the priest, this is a prayer which remembers how Jesus gave thanks at the Last Supper. The events of Jesus's life, death and resurrection are retold.

9. The Communion. God is asked to bless the bread and wine. The Lord's Prayer is said. The words spoken by Jesus at the Last Supper are repeated by the priest. Bread is broken to remember how Jesus's body was broken on the cross. The people come and kneel at the altar rail. Each person is given a piece of bread and a sip of wine.

10. Final Prayer. A final prayer sends people out from the church: 'Go in peace and serve the Lord'.

Salvation Army Worship

Salvation Army worship is often noisy, cheerful and emotional – though there are quiet times for personal testimony. There is no set form of service. Music plays a big part and is particularly important at open-air meetings where it makes an impact that the spoken word cannot. Anyone may lead the worship.

Bible readings are an important part of every meeting and the more modern translations are the most popular.

Emphasis is on individual salvation through faith and personal holiness. These are reflected in the Sunday services. The morning service is called the Holiness Meeting when the Army's teaching ministry to Christians is the main aim. The evening service is called the Salvation meeting and is aimed mainly at non-Christians.

Baptist Worship

There is very little decoration in a Baptist church, and the use of crosses, images, statues and candles is avoided.

A 'minister' is chosen from amongst the people to lead the worship. He or she acts on behalf of the people. He or she will give a sermon during the service.

Prayers are most often spoken spontaneously. Some Baptist churches believe very strongly that worship should be freely guided by the power of the Holy Spirit. Times are left during prayers for people to take part as they are moved by the Spirit. They may 'speak in tongues'.

Lord's Supper services are an important part of Baptist worship and any believer may take the bread and the wine. This sort of service may not be held every week, but at special times of the year.

Pentecostal Worship

Worship is usually led by a minister. Prayers are made up at the time, and taken as a sign that the Spirit is present and working in the people at the service. Modern, lively hymns, often called choruses, are an important part of Pentecostal services.

Pentecostal Christians believe that it is a sign of the presence of the Holy Spirit when people 'speak in tongues'. The language does not seem to have any recognisable words and does not always make sense to the listeners. Pentecostalists think of it as a way of praising God when ordinary words are not enough to express feeling.

The House Church Movement

A growing number of people are part of the House Church Movement. The Christians who belong to these groups base their worship and much of their lives on the practices of the earliest Christians. They meet for worship in ordinary homes, and everyone is important in the group's act of worship.

The group sits in a circle. The bread and a cup of wine are on a table in the centre.

Each group has its own elder, chosen according to directions given in the New Testament.

Sunday evening worship may consist of Bible readings from the New Testament, and there may be a mid-week service of readings from the Old Testament.

Private Worship

Prayer and Meditation

Jesus told his followers to pray individually to God. He said they should not be tempted to show off by praying in public places. He set them an example by often going off by himself to pray to God.

Prayers usually contain four parts, which may be remembered by the mnemonic ACTS:

A = *Adoration*, praising God:

C = *Confession* of wrongdoing, being sorry and asking forgiveness;

T = *Thanksgiving*, thanking God for everything he does;

S = *Supplication*, asking God for support, guidance and comfort for oneself and others.

The Lord's Prayer is the only example of prayer left by Jesus himself. Christians through the centuries have found it helpful to meditate on certain words of the Bible; or on hymns and prayers; or specifically on Jesus, Mary or God.

Christians have also found certain aids useful in fixing their thoughts on God:

A crucifix – a cross with an image of Jesus on it.

Pictures or statues (icons) – of Jesus, Mary or other holy figures.

A rosary – a string of beads from which a crucifix hangs. Roman Catholics use a rosary to recite prayers whilst counting the beads.

Some devout Christians may spend a day or a weekend in 'retreat' at a religious centre like a monastery, where they give their whole attention to prayer and thinking about God. They hope this will refresh and deepen their spiritual life and renew their belief.

Bible Study

Many Christians use the Bible to help them with their private devotion. They may simply read a passage each day or use specially written Bible study notes to help them understand the Bible better as they read it.

6 Pilgrimage

A pilgrimage is a journey to a holy place as an act of devotion. For many Christians, a visit to a place that has special connections with an important person or event in Christian history is inspiring and beneficial. To other Christians, pilgrimage is a journey through life, a pilgrimage of the soul, where faith is strengthened by coping with life's problems. In either case, an effort is required from the Christian. The reward may be great personal development and a more disciplined spiritual life.

Some Christians disapprove of pilgrimages to shrines because:

1. prayers may be offered to the Virgin Mary or other saints;
2. shops may make money out of souvenirs such as statues of Mary.

It has been suggested, however, that the annual conferences of Protestant denominations have some of the characteristics and offer some of the inspirations that others may draw from pilgrimage.

Special Places of Pilgrimage

The Holy Land

For many Christians, the most important place for a pilgrimage is Israel, the Holy Land, the country where Jesus spent his life on earth.

Pilgrims try to include visits to Bethlehem, the birthplace of Jesus; to Nazareth, where he grew up; to the Sea of Galilee, where he spent much of his ministry teaching and healing; and to Jerusalem, where his arrest, trial, crucifixion and resurrection took place.

Jerusalem. It is possible to walk along the route, the Via Dolorosa (the Way of Sorrow), taken by Jesus as he went to his execution at the Place of Golgotha. You can stop at each Station of the Cross – fourteen sites marking the events of Good Friday.

Bethlehem. The stable where Jesus was born is now a huge ornate church, and, at Christmas, Christian denominations take it in turn to hold their own processions and services. The church is always full of guides and tourists.

Europe

Rome. Roman Catholics especially wish to make a pilgrimage to Rome, the city where the Apostles Peter and Paul were said to have been martyred. Roman Catholic Christians believe that Peter was the first Bishop of Rome, and Pope; and that Bishops of Rome have continued the line of leadership from him. Today, the official home of the Pope is the Vatican Palace. There is an enormous church named after the Apostle Peter, known as the Basilica of Saint Peter.

On the major festival days, Christians gather in Saint Peter's Square to hear the Pope's message and receive his blessing. For most pilgrims, the sight of the Pope is the most important part of their visit.

Lourdes. Lourdes is a town in the French Pyrenees. In 1858 a girl named Bernadette Soubirous had a series of visions of the Virgin Mary in the Grotto of Massabiele. She was encouraged by the vision to scratch the earth and a spring of water appeared. The Virgin told her that the spring must be visited by people who needed healing and that the people should go to the spring in procession.

From about 1864 onwards, pilgrimages were organised to the grotto at Lourdes. Many cases of sick people being cured have been reported. Today, there are many large basilicas and the grotto can still be visited. Pilgrims go to Lourdes all the year round. Miraculous cures are still announced, but most pilgrims say that the experience of visiting Lourdes helps them spiritually or emotionally, even though they may not have been cured.

Santiago de Compostela. This city in north-west Spain has been a popular place of pilgrimage since the Middle Ages. There is a story that the Apostle James had preached in Spain after the resurrection of Jesus, and that after James had been martyred in AD 44 his body was taken to Spain for safety. Santiago is Spanish for St. James. A shrine was built over his tomb, but it was forgotten until a stone church was built on the site in the ninth century AD. The tomb of St. James became a rallying-point for Spanish Christians fighting the Moors, and in the Middle Ages Santiago de Compostela became the most important place of pilgrimage after Rome.

Britain. Closer to home, British Christians may make pilgrimages to Knock in Ireland, Iona in the Hebrides, Holy Island off the Northumbrian coast, and Walsingham in Norfolk.

7 Festivals

The major Christian festivals recall events in the life of Jesus. The Christian year begins at Advent, in preparation for the birth of Jesus – 25th December, Christmas Day. This is a fixed date, unlike the festivals of Easter, Ascension and Whitsun which are determined by the movement of the Moon and fall on different dates each year. Orthodox Christians celebrate their festivals a fortnight later than all other Christian denominations.

The Christian Year

Advent

Advent means 'coming' or 'arrival' and is the time of preparation for Christ's birth. It begins on the Sunday nearest to 30th November. There are four Sundays in Advent.

Christmas

The most important part of Christmas for Christians is sharing the celebration of the birth of Jesus with other Christians in church. Christmas hymns and carols are sung, the story of the nativity is read from the Bible, and Communion services are held on Christmas Day. The festival starts on Christmas Eve and lasts for twelve days until the feast of Epiphany on 6th January. Christmas in the Orthodox Church is not celebrated until 6th January.

Customs include:

The Crib. Many homes, schools, shops and churches have models of the stable scene. This is called a crib, and is the only truly Christian custom.

Holly, Mistletoe and Ivy. All evergreens symbolise that even in deepest winter, life is present. The use of evergreens was taken from old pagan celebrations.

The Christmas Tree. A Christian named Boniface introduced the practice of decorating a young fir tree with gifts for the Christ child.

● Christians celebrate Christmas because they believe that God sent his only son into the world to bring his message of light, love, goodness and peace. The token of God's love was Jesus.

Many churches now hold a *Christingle* service, a custom which began in Scandinavia. During the service each child is given a Christingle – a candle set in an orange, with a ribbon round the centre and fruit set on cocktail sticks. All parts of a Christingle have meaning:

Orange – the world;

Candle – Jesus, the Light of the World;

Ribbon – the love of Jesus which goes all round the world;

Fruit – the food with which God always feeds his people.

Epiphany

Originally, Epiphany celebrated both the birth and the baptism of Jesus. Since about AD 300, it has marked especially the visit of the Three Wise Men (Magi) to the stable. Its date is always 6th January. It is sometimes called 'Little Christmas'. Twelfth Night is the evening of 5th January.

Lent

Lent is the time of preparation for Easter. The word means 'spring' and it is a period of forty weekdays lasting from Ash Wednesday to Holy Saturday. It commemorates Jesus's fasting in the wilderness.

Years ago, Lent was kept very strictly. People ate only one meal a day, in the evening. Meat, fish, milk, butter, cheese, eggs were all forbidden, so the one daily meal was very plain. Later, these strict rules were relaxed. The meal was eaten earlier in the day and an evening snack was allowed.

Some Christians still fast during Lent; others give up something which they enjoy, such as sweets, chocolate, cakes, cigarettes or alcohol. Many spend extra time in prayer or Bible study, or make a special effort to help people in need. Roman Catholics are obliged to go to confession during Lent to prepare for Easter.

Shrove Tuesday – *the last day before Lent*. Shrove comes from the word 'shriving', which means confessing sins and being forgiven. Shrove Tuesday is a way for getting rid of old sins and making a new start for Lent in preparation for Easter.

Another name for Shrove Tuesday is *Pancake Tuesday*. Years ago, housewives made pancakes to use up all their eggs, butter and milk before the start of Lent. Pancakes are still eaten on this day, and pancake races are held in some parts of Britain. In New Orleans, USA, a festival called Mardi Gras (Fat Tuesday) includes magnificent processions through the streets on the day before the start of Lent.

Ash Wednesday – *the first day of Lent.* Ash Wednesday takes its name from the practice of putting ashes on one's head as a sign of repentance. At one time, people who had done wrong appeared in public in sackcloth and ashes at the start of the forty-day period of Lent, so they could be forgiven; and they were given bread and wine during Holy Communion services on Easter Day. This custom has died out, but many Christians are marked on the forehead with a cross of cold ash as a sign of penitence and preparation for Easter during a service held in church on Ash Wednesday.

Refreshment Sunday – *the fourth Sunday in Lent.* This is so called because it was a day of refreshment, midway through Lent, when Lenten strictness was relaxed. Simnel cakes (special rich fruit cakes) used to be eaten on this day.

Refreshment Sunday has been transformed into Mothering Sunday, when people buy cards and presents for their mothers. Most do not realise that the day is really a Christian celebration – modern commercialism has obscured its true origins.

Passion Sunday – *the fifth Sunday in Lent.* As Easter draws nearer, Lent becomes more solemn. The last days of Jesus's life (the 'Passion') are thought about in church services. In many churches, the crosses, statues and pictures are draped with black or purple cloth to make the church more sombre and encourage a feeling of sadness.

Holy Week

Holy Week is the last week of Lent, when Christians remember the suffering and death of Jesus. There may be services every day during this week.

Palm Sunday. The Sunday before Easter is Palm Sunday. The Bible tells that Jesus rode into Jerusalem on a donkey and was welcomed by crowds waving palm branches as they went to meet him. Many churches give each member of the congregation a small piece of palm branch, often shaped into a cross. Some denominations have a procession.

Maundy Thursday. Maundy Thursday was the day on which Jesus shared the Last Supper with his disciples. The word *maundy* comes from the Latin word 'mandatum' meaning commandment. Jesus commanded his followers to 'love one another' at this Last Supper.

Good Friday. Good Friday is the anniversary of the day Jesus was crucified. Many churches re-enact the story in their own church. All churches hold a special very solemn service.

In Roman Catholic churches, and some Anglican ones, the Stations of the Cross are used to retrace Christ's journey to his crucifixion, and prayers are said at each Station.

Easter Eve – Saturday. Churches are made ready for the joy of Easter Day; black and purple cloths are removed from the statues and pictures, and the crucifix is replaced by an empty cross. Silver and gold colours appear on the altars, Bible markers and pulpit cloth and in the flowers which decorate the building. Candles are placed ready for the next day.

Easter Day

Easter Day is the most important Christian festival, and always falls on a Sunday. The main services are held during the morning. Some Christians get up at dawn to begin their celebrations.

The Roman Catholic and Orthodox Easter vigils begin very early on Easter Day in remembrance of the time the women came to the tomb. The vigil starts outside the church in the dark: a fire is lit, and a single lighted candle (the Paschal Candle) is carried into the church to represent the resurrected Christ. Other candles are lit from it.

The joyful words 'Christ is Risen, Alleluia!' are exchanged by Christians. The empty cross tells its own story. The Bible is read and hymns are sung.

● The word Easter comes from the pagan goddess Eostre, whose name meant 'the dawn'. Her festival was celebrated every spring.

● For Christians, Easter is about the resurrection of Jesus, the conquering of death for all time. It is a festival which offers Christians the hope that they, too, will be resurrected.

● The Jewish festival of Passover (Pesach) tells how the Jews were saved by the blood of a lamb. Christians believe that Jesus saves them from sin and death. To Christians, Jesus is the Lamb of God. Lamb is often part of a traditional Easter meal and lambs are well known symbols of Easter, linking the title given to Jesus with the theme of continuing life.

● Eggs are an easily recognised symbol of continued life and resurrection, used centuries before the first Easter Day.

Ascension Day

Ascension Day is celebrated on the Thursday forty days after Easter Sunday, and is a day which enables Christians to celebrate the victory of Jesus over death and his continuing life. It is the day Jesus was taken up (Acts 1,9) to his rightful place in heaven beside God. He is spoken of as

'Christ the King' or 'Christ in Majesty' on this day.

There are no special celebrations except that services, especially Holy Communion, are held in churches. The Paschal Candle is extinguished for the last time.

Whitsun or Pentecost

Whit Sunday is the seventh Sunday after Easter and commemorates the descent of the Holy Spirit at Pentecost. For fifty days after the crucifixion, the disciples had hidden away in the Upper Room where the Last Supper had taken place. On the fiftieth day (Pentecost), the Holy Spirit gave them the courage to go out and preach to the world (Acts 2).

The name Whitsun simply comes from the words 'White Sunday'. This was the day on which people were baptised into the Christian faith if they had not been baptised at Easter. Newly baptised Christians wore or were given white clothes as a sign of their new faith.

Sunday

Sunday is the day most Christians meet for worship. It is also known as the Christian holy day of rest, the Christian Sabbath. Jews call Saturday the Sabbath and have obeyed God's commandment to keep this day holy. Early Christians kept Saturday as the Sabbath but soon began to think of Sunday, the day Jesus had risen from the dead, as being more special. They also remembered that it was the day God started his creation. As Christianity separated from Judaism, Saturday became less and less important and Sunday became the Christian holy day.

• In some Christian traditions, especially some Protestant denominations, all work is still forbidden on Sundays.

8 Rites of Passage

The Seven Sacraments

Important stages in the lives of Christians may be marked by religious ceremonies. These are known as *sacraments*. A sacrament is a visible action or sequence of actions with an invisible, spiritual meaning. Until the Reformation, all Christians recognised that there were seven sacraments:

1. Baptism. Water symbolises the washing-away of sin. New life is received inwardly through the grace of the Holy Spirit.

2. Confirmation. The Bishop's hands laid on people symbolise the confirming of the grant of the Holy Spirit which occurred at baptism.

3. Communion. The bread and wine symbolise receiving Jesus, and strengthen a feeling of union with him.

4. Ordination. The laying-on of hands with prayer by a Bishop are symbols of handing on authority and power to perform the work of a priest.

5. Marriage. A ring is given as a symbol of eternal love between the couple.

6. Reconciliation. A person can confess sins to God in the presence of a priest and perform a penance. Words of pardon or absolution are then spoken, assuring a Christian of God's forgiveness.

7. Anointing of the Sick. A sick or dying person is anointed with Holy Oil and blessed by a priest as a symbol of receiving God's grace.

These seven sacraments are no longer universally recognised.

● The Orthodox and Roman Catholic traditions still recognise all seven sacraments.

● Anglican and other Protestant churches recognise baptism and Holy Communion as the only two sacraments which were instituted by Jesus himself.

● Other denominations may not use the word sacrament, but they recognise the importance of the ideas contained in them.

Baptism

The New Testament tells how Jesus was himself baptised by John the Baptist. The last words of Jesus to his followers were: 'Therefore go and make disciples of all nations, baptising them in the name of the Father and of the Son and of the Holy Spirit.' (Matthew 28,19-20).

Since that time, baptism has been the first stage in becoming a Christian for every denomination except Quakers, Baptists and the

Salvation Army. Some churches baptise babies; others prefer people to make their own decisions later in life.

Dedication

Christians who do not practise infant baptism may take their baby to church for a service of dedication. They believe that baptism is such an important step that it should take place only when a person is old enough to understand its purpose and meaning, and the person asks to be baptised.

Dedication allows parents to thank God for the gift of a child, and parents are given a certificate to mark the dedication service.

Believer's Baptism

Once someone has made a personal decision to be baptised, he or she attends classes to make sure the commitment to be made at baptism is fully understood. Believer's baptism is usually by total immersion in water, either in a river, a swimming-bath or a specially built tank in church. After the ceremony the person receives a certificate of baptism.

Confirmation

Except in the Orthodox tradition, Churches which baptise infants recognise that children need to make for themselves the promises made on their behalf at baptism. This usually means taking part in another service in church which allows them to confirm their faith in public. In the Anglican and Roman Catholic traditions, the service is called Confirmation.

Roman Catholics may be confirmed from the age of seven onwards. Anglicans are usually confirmed from about twelve onwards.

The service includes:

1. the laying-on of hands by a bishop;

2. the persons to be confirmed making for themselves the answers and promises made on their behalf at baptism.

Making a First Communion

In many denominations, Holy Communion may only be received by people who have been baptised and confirmed. In the Orthodox tradition, all three (baptism, confirmation and first communion) take place in infancy during the same ceremony. Roman Catholic children may be allowed to receive their first communion at about the age of seven, before confirmation. In some Free Churches, people may receive bread and wine before becoming full Church members. Churches practising believer's baptism consider that this represents full membership.

Marriage

The Christian faith sets a high value on marriage and family life. There are a variety of reasons for this.

- Marriage is for the procreation of children.
- Marriage provides the right relationship for sexual intercourse.
- Marriage gives the couple mutual companionship, help and comfort.
- Family life was created by God and made firm by Jesus.
- Children are taught about God in the family.
- Jesus was born into and grew up in a family.
- Family members have a responsibility to care for one another.
- There are obligations for both parents and children if family life is to function well.

Christians believe that the proper basis for marriage is the love of the partners for each other, and that the man and the woman are equal partners in marriage.

Strictly speaking, the marriage should be for life (Mark 10,1-9), though legal grounds for divorce have recently been widened and it is now much easier to get a divorce. It is not always easy for a divorced person whose former partner is still living, to be remarried in the Church of England. For Roman Catholics the marriage vows can never be broken, so divorce is not recognised. In some cases, legal separation may be necessary, but the couple remain married and cannot marry anyone else. Annulments are sometimes granted in cases where the vows are considered never to have been valid.

Many Christians believe that God's blessing on a marriage should be available to anyone who wishes to have it. Others think a regular commitment to the Church is required, but few ministers refuse to marry non-churchgoers. They will try to make them see the importance of the ceremony's religious element, and help them to see beyond the excitement of the other preparations.

Relationships within Marriage

The bridegroom is compared to Christ and the bride to the Church. As Christ is head of the body (people) of the Church, so the husband is head of the family. Until recently, women had to promise to *obey* their husbands. They may now choose to promise to *cherish* instead.

A Christian Marriage Ceremony

The ceremony consists of promises before witnesses, with prayers

and blessings by a leader of the congregation. The form the marriage service takes depends on the denomination to which the couple belong.

Christian marriage ceremonies usually have six parts:

1. a statement of the purpose of marriage;
2. questions asked of bride and groom to make sure they can legally be married;
3. questions asked of them to confirm their wish to marry;
4. the actual marriage – exchange of vows and rings;
5. declaration that in God's eyes they are married;
6. prayers asking God to help them to stay faithful, and to help them throughout their married life, and asking for God's blessing.

Death

Most Christians would agree that because Jesus died on the cross and rose from the dead three days later, death is not something to be frightened of – Jesus was victorious over death.

Christians are encouraged to think of a funeral service as a ceremony in which they remind themselves of their essential beliefs. They should become aware that their faith in God will help them to face the sorrow which the death of a loved one has brought.

Most people do need a ritual to mark the separation from a loved one. It is a way of 'letting go' and eases the separation of the bereaved from the dead. The time between the death and the funeral is a means of transition, moving to the re-entry into ordinary everyday life after the committal. Re-entry into the home is a symbol of this re-entry.

An Orthodox Funeral

When an Orthodox Christian dies, the body is washed and then dressed in new clothes as an outward sign of the new life which

Christians look for beyond the grave. Psalms and prayers for the dead are read over the body.

At the funeral, the deceased lies in the centre of the church, in front of the altar. The coffin is usually open so that the body is in full view. Four candlesticks are placed at the sides of the coffin to form a cross. The mourners hold lighted candles as a sign that the dead person's life has not been extinguished.

The order of the service reminds everyone of the day Jesus rose from the dead. The church is full of lights. There are burning candles and incense, symbols of life and prayer. The Bible readings emphasise eternal life and the resurrection of Christ.

A Roman Catholic Funeral

In recent years there have been changes in the Roman Catholic funeral. The central theme now is the resurrection of Christ. The emphasis is not on fear or grief or loss, but on God's faithfulness and the Christian hope. After the service comes the final commendation and farewell, and the committal, where, after a short and simple rite, the body is lowered into the grave. Alternatively, the Roman Catholic church now permits cremation.

An Anglican Funeral

On the day of the funeral, the body is taken to the church in a coffin. The coffin is carried or wheeled to the top of the church. Close family members follow the coffin and take up the front seats in the church.

The vicar then leads a service consisting of:

- A hymn.
- A Bible reading.
- The eulogy. This will remind the congregation of the good things the dead person did in life.
- The vicar may then read some of the words from the Te Deum Laudamus, a prayer on behalf of the dead person, asking Jesus to make sure he or she goes to heaven.
- Prayers. Thanks are given for the life of the dead person, and God is asked to comfort the bereaved.
- Hymn. The final hymn may possibly be a favourite of the dead person.
- Benediction. The vicar says the benediction:

'The grace of our Lord Jesus Christ, and the love of God, and the fellowship of the Holy Spirit, be with you all, Amen.'
The coffin will be carried out of the church and taken to the graveyard.

- The committal at the graveside. The mourners gather round as the coffin is lowered into the ground.

As the words 'ashes to ashes, dust to dust' are said, a handful of dust is thrown into the grave, which is filled later.

Cremation

Many Christians now choose cremation rather than burial. The whole funeral may take place at the crematorium, which is like a small chapel. The coffin is often placed on a platform in front of the mourners. The ceremony is usually shorter than a church ceremony, but follows the same pattern.

After the service, instead of the graveside committal the coffin is removed to where the body is cremated. The ashes of the dead person can either be held in a container at the crematorium or buried privately elsewhere.

Cremation is not practised by some Protestant groups.

SECTION 2: Contemporary Issues in Christian Perspectives

Introduction

This section of the book deals with Christian responses to the numerous social and personal issues encountered in the modern world, and shows how aspects of these issues relate to biblical teaching.

This is such a wide-ranging topic that it is only possible to cover the basic facts and principles involved in each issue. Students should remember that they will have to be aware of both Christian and secular responses to contemporary issues, and for this reason religious and non-religious views have been included.

9 Morality and Ethics

What is Morality?

Morality is the consideration of the patterns of conduct and rules for right and wrong behaviour. A moral decision is made when the individual decides which form of conduct will be morally correct. People may disagree about what form of behaviour is right and what is wrong.

Free Will

Free will is the belief that moral actions are the result of a free choice of how to behave. Some people believe that they make their choice of how to behave after they have considered the consequences of their action according to their moral consciousness.

Determinism

Other individuals believe that moral decisions are made as a result of the major influences on them during their life, such as the environment in which they grew up, their physical and psychological make-up, and the attitudes of the society in which they live. Determinism is the belief that moral actions are determined by external influences.

What is Ethics?

Ethics is the study of morality, of human actions in respect of right and wrong conduct. Many different concepts have been put forward by philosophers to try to solve the problem of knowing how to behave in a moral way in any situation.

Egoism

Egoists believe that each person should act in the way which will benefit that person the most. However, this theory of self-interest is unlikely to work, since other people are bound to suffer if each individual follows only his or her own inclinations. It will therefore not benefit the individual to turn everyone against them, so other people's interests will need to be taken into account.

Hedonism

The Greek philosopher Epicurus taught that the main aim in life should be to seek pleasure for the physical and spiritual self. Hedonists believe that only actions which bring pleasure may be considered good, and therefore moral, whereas actions which bring pain are evil, and therefore immoral.

Utilitarianism

This doctrine states that the main aim of all humans is happiness, and it maintains that actions are made morally right or wrong according to their good or bad consequences. A familiar definition is that actions are right in so far as they promote happiness or pleasure.

Utilitarianism is associated with Jeremy Bentham (1748-1832) and John Stuart Mill (1806-73). They promoted the 'greatest happiness' principle to bring about legal and social change in order to bring harmony by challenging the motive of self-interest. A utilitarian would judge an action as morally right or wrong in terms of the amount of happiness produced by that action. However, this may allow an action which is right on utilitarian grounds – because it promotes the greatest happiness for the greatest number – to be judged wrong on other moral grounds.

Christian Ethics

Christian ethics looks to the teaching of the New Testament and the Church as a guide to how to behave in a moral way according to God's will. A Christian can show love of God only by loving mankind. This ethic stresses the claim of the needs of others before our own needs. This concern for others is Christian love (agape), and this love consists of caring for all people, whoever they are and whatever they may have done wrong. It is the motive behind an action, together with the action itself, which should be judged as right or wrong.

10 Crime and Punishment

Crime

Rules are necessary to guide and control behaviour. When all the people in a country are expected to keep a rule, and can be punished if they break it, then the rule is called a law. Such a law is intended to protect society from those who wish to do harm, and to break that law is a crime.

A crime is a social act that offends the laws of society. Each society has a set of laws, and when these laws are broken the person who breaks them is a criminal.

Crimes may be divided into two categories:
1. against property – e.g. theft and vandalism;
2. against people – e.g. assault, rape and murder.

When God's laws (e.g. the Ten Commandments) are broken, it is a sin. Sins are punished by God.

The Causes of Crime

The most common causes of crime are:

Greed – the criminal wants what others possess.

Lack of parental guidance – the criminal was never taught the difference between right and wrong.

Addiction – a person breaks the law under the influence of drugs or alcohol, or to pay for an addiction.

Boredom – the criminal wants some excitement in life.

Revenge – criminals want to get their own back on an individual or on society.

Mental illness – the person cannot control his or her behaviour.

Poverty – the criminal wants something but cannot afford it.

Unemployment – the criminal resorts to crime in the absence of work.

Punishment

The Aims of Punishment

The Theory of Vindication states that if crimes are not punished, then the laws of a country are pointless. If laws are to be respected, crimes must be punished. There are four different aims of punishment: retribution, deterrence, protection and reformation.

- **Retribution.** The aim of retribution is to take revenge on criminals for their actions, to make them suffer for their crimes.
- **Deterrence.** The aim of deterrence is twofold – to stop criminals from repeating their crimes and, by making an example of the criminal, to stop others from committing similar crimes.
- **Protection.** Protection aims at safeguarding society from criminal acts. The criminal's freedom is limited so that he or she finds it difficult to repeat the crime.
- **Reformation.** The aim of this punishment is to reform criminals so that they no longer want to commit crimes.

Forms of Punishment

The punishment chosen should reflect the severity of the crime, as well as taking into consideration any previous convictions the offender has, his or her mental state, and the environment from which the offender comes.

Punishments may take the following forms:

- **Imprisonment.** Offenders are sent to prison for any term from a few hours to 'life'. The sentence is imposed by the court, after all the facts in a case have been considered.
- **Fine.** The offender has to pay money to the court. The amount paid depends on the offence committed.
- **Disqualification.** The offender is banned from doing something for a set period of time – for example, banned from driving because of involvement in a serious accident.
- **Community service.** The offender has to do unpaid work in the community (e.g. gardening for the elderly or repairing public property) for a set number of hours.

The Christian Attitude to Offenders

Christ's teaching makes it clear that Christians will be forgiven by God if they are truly sorry and turn back to him, and have shown forgiveness of others. If God is willing to forgive us and offer us a second chance, we must treat offenders in the same way.

'Thou Shalt Not Kill' (Matthew 5,21-26)

Jesus states that not only those who kill will be punished but also those who are angry, because anger is a motive which can lead to murder.

Christians who show anger are not living together in harmony. Therefore, before going to worship God, all quarrels must be ended. Similarly, Christians should not behave in such a way that they are brought before the courts. If such an action is necessary, Christians are not living as God wishes.

The Parable of the Unmerciful Servant (Matthew 18,23-35)

This parable teaches that as God (the master) forgives us (the servant) the major sins, so we must forgive others (the fellow-servant) the smaller sins they have done against us. If we do not show such forgiveness, God will punish us (the Master in the parable throws the servant into jail).

The Parable of the Prodigal Son (Luke 15,11-32)

The father (God) welcomes back the younger son (a sinner) who is sorry and has returned to him. If God can welcome back sinners, we must not be self-righteous like the older brother and think that because we have never done wrong we deserve better treatment than those who have strayed and returned.

The Penitent Thief (Luke 23,32-43)

Jesus is crucified on the Cross between two criminals. One mocks him, but the other realises that they have done wrong and deserve punishment, whereas Jesus is innocent. The criminal's regret for his own misdeeds and his realisation of Jesus's power meant that he, too, would be saved. In the same way, we can achieve salvation by turning to Christ.

A Woman Taken in Adultery (John 8,1-11)

A woman was brought before Jesus for committing adultery. The lawyers, wishing to catch Jesus out, asked him if she should be stoned – the penalty for such a crime, set by Moses. Jesus replied that only those free of sin can condemn others. Only God is perfect, therefore only God can make such a judgement. As we are all sinners, we must forgive other people and seek to reform them by giving them a second chance.

'Vengeance is Mine' (Romans 12,14-21)

Here, Paul is repeating Christ's teaching that revenge is to be left to God. We must try to help our enemies, even feeding them if they are hungry. In this way, we are doing what is God's will and making our enemies even more aware of their own misdeeds.

Capital Punishment

Capital punishment is the death penalty. The aim of capital punishment may be retribution, deterrence, protection, or a combination of all three.

Arguments in Favour of Capital Punishment

1. The death penalty acts as a deterrent. Since the abolition of capital punishment in Britain in 1965, there has been an increase in violent crime.

2. When there was a death penalty, criminals were less inclined to carry weapons, so there was less risk of people being killed during crimes.

3. Execution removes the risk of the criminal repeating the crime.

4. Society is better off without such criminals. The money saved from paying for their upkeep in prison could be used to help others in need.

5. Execution is more humane than a life sentence. Some prisoners have even requested execution (e.g. Gary Gilmore in the USA).

6. Execution is the only punishment which reflects society's horror at certain types of crime. It stops members of the public from taking the law into their own hands.

7. People should keep God's laws. Genesis states: 'Whoever sheds the blood of a man, by man shall his blood be shed; for God made man in his own image.'

8. Moses instructed 'An eye for an eye, a tooth for a tooth and a life for a life'. Execution is the only punishment which meets this demand in the case of murder.

Arguments Against Capital Punishment

1. Execution is a barbaric and outdated practice in modern society. 'Vengeance is mine, says the Lord'; humans should not take life. The abolition of the death penalty shows progress as a civilised society.

2. An innocent person may be executed for a crime he or she did not commit. This has happened in the past, e.g. Timothy Evans.

3. Eighty per cent of murders are not premeditated, therefore offenders do not stop to consider the consequences of their actions. The death penalty does not act as a deterrent in such cases.

4. The sixth commandment states, 'Thou shalt not kill', yet society would have a paid executioner.

5. The teaching of Jesus emphasised that we must show forgiveness and seek to reform people.

6. The death penalty punishes not only criminals but also their families, since they lose a loved one.

7. In the case of terrorism, the death penalty would increase the risk of violence. Terrorists would see execution as a way of becoming martyrs to their cause. On the day of execution, reprisals could be taken involving the killing of innocent people.

11 Decisions of Life and Living

Christians believe that each person is created in God's image, and therefore human life is sacred. However, Christians are divided in their opinion as to when life begins, and this has resulted in differences of opinion on such matters as contraception and abortion. This chapter also covers the Christian views of pre-marital sex and marriage.

Contraception

Contraception refers to the various methods which couples use to try to avoid unwanted pregnancies.

Some contraceptives are artificial, such as the Pill, which is taken by women to control their hormones so that they do not become pregnant. Other methods of contraception are seen as 'natural' – that is, these methods are part of God's Creation. The 'rhythm method' is one example. A woman is at her most fertile immediately before and after ovulation, so to avoid conception, sexual intercourse is best avoided on those days. The other days of her cycle are considered safe.

All Christian Churches believe that through sexual intercourse, a husband and wife express their love for each other and become one. Children are a product of that love only if the couple want them.

Christians sometimes disagree over the purpose and meaning of sexual intercourse, and as a result have different opinions about contraception.

The Roman Catholic and Greek Orthodox Churches teach that the main purpose of the sex act is reproduction. The instruction in Genesis is to 'be fruitful and multiply', so if a couple have sex but try to avoid producing a child, they are committing a sin because they are going against this divine instruction. These Churches believe that only natural methods of birth control are acceptable, because they have been established by God.

Protestant Churches teach that the use of contraception is acceptable within marriage so long as both partners agree.

Abortion

Abortion is the ending of pregnancy before birth, either by natural means (miscarriage) or by an operation to cause it (procured or induced abortion).

The Abortion Act 1967

Since the 1967 Abortion Act, an abortion may be legally prescribed in Britain if two doctors agree that in consequence of the continuation of the pregnancy, the pregnant woman is likely to incur one of the following risks:

- The continuation of the pregnancy risks the life of the woman.
- The pregnant woman's physical or mental health will be at risk if the pregnancy continues.
- A further child would put at risk the physical or mental health of the pregnant woman's existing children.
- There is a serious risk that the child will be born with a physical or mental handicap.

The abortion must be performed by a registered doctor in a recognised hospital.

The 1967 Abortion Act allowed the abortion to be performed before the 28th week of pregnancy. This was the age at which it was felt that a child could survive outside the womb. As scientific advances have enabled babies as young as 21 weeks to survive, it was felt that there needed to be a change in the law. The Human Fertilisation and Embryology Bill 1990 amended the 1967 Abortion Act. An abortion must now be performed before the 24th week of pregnancy. However, an abortion is allowed up to birth if it is to prevent grave permanent injury to the physical or mental health of the mother, or if there is substantial risk that the child will be seriously disabled.

Arguments in Favour of Abortion

People who support abortion, such as The Abortion Reform Group, put forward the following arguments:

- A women should have the right to choose what happens to her body.
- If legalised abortions become more difficult, there would be an increase in the number of illegal abortions, and resulting deaths.
- It is wrong to bring an unwanted child into the world, especially if that child is also handicapped. Unwanted children may suffer rejection and this could create problems for society.
- When pregnancy is the result of rape or sexual abuse, the woman should not be forced to continue with the pregnancy.
- Independent life does not begin until the end of the pregnancy. An abortion destroys only a foetus, a collection of cells, which cannot survive outside the mother before the 24th week of pregnancy.
- If the mother is at risk of dying, or of being handicapped, then her survival is of greater importance than that of the foetus, especially if she already has children needing her care.

Arguments Against Abortion

Organisations such as the Society for the Protection of the Unborn Child (SPUC) and Life put forward arguments against the present abortion law. These include:

- The unborn child is alive from the moment of conception and has rights, including the right to life.
- If abortions are easily obtained, they may be used as another form of contraception, thus encouraging *promiscuity* (sleeping around).
- Twenty-four weeks is too late to perform an abortion; the woman's dates may be wrong and the foetus that is aborted may have a chance of survival. Abortion then becomes infanticide.
- Many couples would welcome the chance to adopt an unwanted baby, but abortions have reduced the number of babies available for adoption.
- There are physical and mental risks for the woman who has an abortion. The operation may lead to sterility, and many women suffer guilt and depression which in some cases has resulted in suicide.

The Christian Position on Abortion

Christians believe that God is the giver of life, so only God has the right to end life. Human life is sacred and cannot be treated in a casual way. The question which Christians have to answer is: when does life begin?

The Roman Catholic Church believes that life begins at the moment of conception and everyone has a right to life, so an abortion is considered as murder. Abortion breaks the commandment 'You shall not kill.'

Anglicans believe that life does not begin until the baby has a chance of surviving independently of its mother; that is to say, at about 24 weeks.

Christians for Free Choice is an organisation of Christians who believe that the matter should be left to an individual's conscience. The decision to continue a pregnancy should not be forced on women.

Many Christians believe that in certain circumstances, such as rape, abortions are morally justifiable. However, they do not believe that abortion should ever be seen as a method of birth control.

Pre-Marital Sex

Christians accept that God instituted sex at the time of Creation. Through sexual intercourse in marriage, a man and a woman express their total commitment to each other for life, and become 'one flesh'. Sex outside marriage goes against God's plan.

Pre-marital sex may not have total commitment or love. It may be a casual relationship which is embarked upon merely to satisfy a physical desire. Such a relationship could be distressing if it resulted in an unwanted pregnancy. Casual sex can lead to a higher risk of catching sexually transmitted diseases, including Aids.

I Corinthians 6,12-20

Paul warns Christians about using their bodies for 'sexual immorality'. Such pleasures are of no lasting value, as our physical form will die and decay. Christians should be concerned about the life everlasting which can be achieved through spiritual unity with Christ. Such a unity can only be harmed by casual sex, because it makes our bodies unclean as a place for the Holy Spirit to enter.

Paul also explains in I Corinthians 3,16-17, that our bodies are God's temple and must be kept undefiled or God will destroy us.

Marriage

Christians believe that sex should take place only between people who are married, and that marriage should be for life. This means that a couple must think carefully about whether they are able to make this lifetime commitment.

Ephesians 5,21-33

Paul teaches that in marriage the wife must accept her husband's decisions. A wife must respect her husband and obey him. However, husbands must love their wives as they love themselves. The relationship between a husband and wife should be the same as that between Christ and his Church – a unity of love, with Christ (the husband) as head.

Differences Between a Christian Marriage Ceremony and a Civil One

There are the following differences between Christian and civil marriage ceremonies.

a) The Christian ceremony takes place in a place of worship, whereas the civil ceremony is performed in a Register Office.

b) The Christian ceremony is a religious ceremony with prayers and hymns, officiated over by a representative of God. A civil ceremony is performed by a representative of the State, and, unless specifically requested by the couple, does not refer to God.

c) The vows in a religious ceremony are made before God, and the couple vow to be faithful for life. Such a requirement is not needed in a civil ceremony.

Why More People Choose a Civil Ceremony

More civil ceremonies are performed each year in Britain than religious ones. Some of the main reasons why people prefer a civil ceremony are:

a) One or other of the partners, or both, may be divorced, and therefore a Church wedding is not permitted.

b) The couple may be of different faiths and unable to decide on the place of worship in which to marry, so they choose a civil ceremony instead.

c) The couple may not be churchgoers and therefore feel that it is hypocritical to make their vows before God.

The Family

The family meets human needs of love and companionship. It provides an economic unit in which everyone is supported, including the children, the sick and the old. A new family unit is created when a man and a woman marry.

The basic unit of the family is found in all societies, and most children are raised in a family group. The organisation of the family varies from society to society and from family to family. Each family has its own rules and ways of doing things.

The family may be divided into two broad groups:

a) The Nuclear Family which usually comprises two adults of opposite sexes, living with their own or adopted children;

b) The Extended Family which includes the nuclear family, together with other close relatives such as grandparents, aunts, uncles and cousins.

Adultery

Adultery takes place when a married person has sexual intercourse with someone other than his or her partner.

Jesus taught in the Sermon on the Mount (Matthew 5,27-30) that not only is adultery wrong, but even to look at someone lustfully is to go against God's wishes. A couple should be faithful to each other for life, both in body and in spirit. Adultery is another means by which the body as a 'temple of God' may be destroyed.

David and Bathsheba (2 Samuel 11)

This Old Testament story is a warning about the dangers of adultery.

Bathsheba is expecting King David's child. Her husband Uriah has been away fighting, so he knows that his wife is guilty of adultery and that he could therefore have her killed as an adulteress. The king engineers Uriah's death and marries Bathsheba, but their child subsequently dies.

The parable which the prophet Nathan told King David shows that the use of power to further one's own desires goes against God's wishes. The story also teaches that adultery brings unhappiness and destroys relationships.

Divorce

Divorce is the legal termination of a marriage. In Britain, one in three marriages ends in divorce. One third of all divorces take place within the first five years of marriage.

The person seeking a divorce is known as the *petitioner*, and the person from whom the divorce is being sought is called the *respondent*.

The Matrimonial Causes Act 1973

This Act stated that in future the *irretrievable breakdown* of a marriage was to be the only grounds for a divorce. To prove irretrievable breakdown – that is, to show that there is no hope of a couple coming back together – evidence of one of five factors must be offered.

1. Adultery. The adultery of one partner has made the marriage intolerable for the other partner.

2. Unreasonable behaviour – either mental or physical cruelty – by one partner.

3. Desertion by one partner for at least two years.

4. Separation for two years. If a couple have lived apart for two years, a divorce can be obtained provided both parties agree.

5. Separation for five years. Where only one partner seeks a divorce, a couple must have lived apart for five years before a divorce can be granted.

The Christian Position on Divorce

The Christian Churches see it as one of their duties to help couples to overcome problems within their marriage, in order to avoid the need for a divorce.

Jesus taught that marriage is a divine institution established by God at the time of Creation. When a man takes a wife, they become 'one flesh'. Only God can end this union.

Jesus seems to suggest (Matthew 5,31-32) that a couple

who can no longer live together may separate, and even divorce, but they may not remarry. If husband and wife separate, and either of them takes another partner, they are guilty of adultery.

The Christian Church is divided on its attitude to whether or not divorced people should be allowed to remarry in church.

The Roman Catholic Church believes that marriage is a sacrament, which may only be ended by God with the death of one partner. Therefore, a divorced person who took marriage vows in the Roman Catholic Church may not remarry in church so long as his or her first partner lives.

The Church of England regards divorce as the last resort. The Anglican Church will recognise a separation on the grounds of irretrievable breakdown of the marriage. However, if a couple divorce, the Church teaches that they may not remarry in church.

Some Anglican clergy are prepared to remarry divorced people in their church, but permission must first be obtained from their bishop. Most clergy will perform a 'blessing' on the second marriage after a civil ceremony.

The Free Churches also look upon divorce as a last resort, but if it does take place, a marriage is regarded as dead. Each couple will be considered individually, and a decision will be made on whether to allow a second marriage before God. For example, many of the clergy in the Free Churches believe that Jesus allowed divorce on the grounds of adultery (Matthew 5,32), and they therefore permit the 'innocent' partner in that marriage to remarry in church.

The Eastern Orthodox Church will agree to the end of a marriage in circumstances such as adultery or desertion.

Suicide

Suicide is the intentional taking of one's own life. In Britain, suicide has been legal since 1961.

The Causes of Suicide

There are many reasons why people wish to commit suicide. The major causes can be outlined as follows:

- A person may be suffering from a severe depressive illness which makes him or her feel alone and unloved. To go on living seems pointless.
- A person may have a terminal illness, with increasing pain or handicap, so it seems better to end life before the suffering increases or before the person becomes a burden to others.
- The loss of a loved one may cause a person to feel that life is no longer worth living.
- Unemployment causes some people to feel that life has no purpose and they are letting everyone down, particularly if increasing debts are a problem.
- Addiction to drugs or alcohol is a potential cause of suicide because the addiction increases feelings of depression.

Christian Attitudes to Suicide

Christians believe that a life given by God should only be taken by God. Most Christians accept that suicide is often the result of the balance of the mind being disturbed by mental or physical distress, and so the individual should not be treated as a criminal. Christians have a duty to help those in need.

In a Christian society, there should always be those who will listen to other people's problems and try to help. The Samaritans is one such organisation.

Euthanasia

Euthanasia means 'easy death', but it is often called 'mercy killing'.

The principle behind euthanasia is that anyone who is terminally ill or in constant pain, or who finds life unacceptable because of age or handicap, should have the right to have his or her life terminated. In Britain, the Voluntary Euthanasia Society (Exit) exists to try to change the law so that euthanasia will become legal.

Since euthanasia is illegal in most countries, medical practitioners can sometimes be placed in a dilemma. For example, a doctor may give a patient a gradually increasing dose of a drug which keeps pain at bay but which may also shorten life as a result. This is sometimes known as passive euthanasia, but it is debatable whether it is euthanasia at all.

This type of euthanasia may also occur when a doctor takes no action to prolong the life of a patient who is terminally ill or severely handicapped – for example, the doctor does not try to resuscitate a patient after a heart attack.

Active euthanasia would take place if a doctor took a deliberate action to terminate a patient's life – for example, by giving a lethal dose of a drug.

Arguments in Favour of Euthanasia

● Supporters of euthanasia argue that every human being should have the right to decide when to die.

● Euthanasia would allow someone who is on a life-support machine, or terminally ill, to die with dignity.

● It is wrong to preserve life artificially beyond its natural span: 'For everything there is a season, and a time for every matter under heaven: a time to be born, and a time to die.' (Ecclesiastes 3,1-2).

● Keeping people alive by machine is not true life, so it is better to allow them to die.

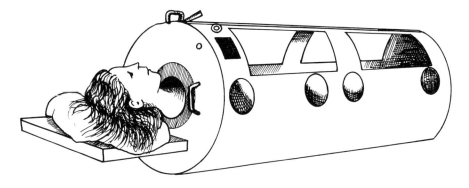

● Suicide is legal, so why not allow people to assist those wishing to die?

● Euthanasia would allow people to die with their family and friends around them in a loving atmosphere, with all their affairs in order.

● It is not death but the process of dying that most people are afraid of. Euthanasia would take away the fear of a painful end to life.

● People would be spared the agony of watching their loved ones suffer a slow, lingering death.

● Animals are not made to suffer if they are in great pain or terminally ill, so the same compassion should be shown to humans.

● Painkillers such as morphine gradually reduce a patient's life span, so why not allow doctors to give one large dose to terminate life?

Arguments Against Euthanasia

- Many Christians oppose the practice of euthanasia because life comes from God and only God has the right to end it.
- Euthanasia goes against the commandment, 'You shall not kill'.
- Paul taught that people must expect suffering in life and should not try to escape from it.
- In parables such as 'The Sheep and the Goats', Jesus teaches that Christians will be judged on how they have helped the sick. Helping the sick, the handicapped and the old teaches compassion, and offers the chance to put Christian teaching into practice.
- Hospices provide a caring environment where terminally-ill patients can die a dignified and painless death, surrounded by love and compassion, so there is no need for euthanasia.
- In 1 Kings 19, the prophet Elijah is depressed and asks God to take his life. God tells Elijah that he still has work for him to do. In the same way, God may still have work for us to do, therefore it is wrong to contemplate euthanasia.
- The doctor's diagnosis might be wrong. A patient given only a few weeks to live may live for years, or may not have a terminal disease at all.
- Euthanasia removes all chance of a cure.
- The doctor/patient relationship will be changed. Doctors take the Hippocratic Oath to preserve life, but if euthanasia were legalised, patients may not believe that the doctor is doing everything possible to cure them.
- 'The body is the temple of God.' Euthanasia therefore is likened to destroying the temple of God.

12 Prejudice and Discrimination

Prejudice

Prejudice is a biased opinion against something or someone for no logical reason, and is formed without real knowledge of the thing or person. Often, prejudice arises out of stereotyping, which is having a fixed mental image about a group of people, based on the belief that all members of a group conform to the same pattern.

Discrimination

Discrimination occurs when an individual or a group is treated differently because of prejudice. For example, people who are discriminated against may be refused service in shops, or may not be given equal opportunities in education, housing or employment.

Racial prejudice occurs when people practise discrimination against particular racial groups.

Causes of Racial Prejudice

It is not always easy to understand why people are prejudiced against a particular race, but the commonest reasons are these:

● Humans tend to form into groups, and to consider anyone who is not in the group an 'enemy' and a threat to their way of life.

● Immigrants come from a different culture and usually speak a different language. This may lead to misunderstandings between the immigrants and the resident population, and the belief that the immigrants are inferior.

● Children learn colour prejudice by the idea that black is evil, through such words as black-hearted, blackmail, and black magic, whereas white is seen as the colour of purity and goodness.

● In times of unemployment there may be tension between racial groups, because one group fears the other is taking its jobs.

- Racial groups are often used as scapegoats. When something goes wrong within a country, the blame may be placed on particular racial groups.

Racial Discrimination and the Law in Britain

The Race Relations Act 1976

Black immigrants who came to Britain found that they did not receive the same treatment as the white population. The Race Relations Act 1976 made discrimination unlawful on grounds of colour, race, nationality or ethnic origin, in the following spheres:

- Employment and training;
- Housing;
- Education;
- Goods, services and facilities;
- Advertising.

The Commission for Racial Equality was set up by the 1976 Act, to work towards ending discrimination and to promote equality of opportunity and good relations between different racial groups.

It is now illegal in Britain to discriminate directly or indirectly. Direct discrimination occurs when people are treated less favourably because of their race or colour, or are segregated because of their race or colour.

Indirect discrimination is to apply a requirement or a condition which affects one racial group adversely. For example, an advertisement for a cleaner may state that the applicant must have a high standard of English, when in fact the ability to speak English does not affect the applicant's ability to do the job.

It is also against the law to publish or, in a public place, to use, language which is threatening, abusive or insulting and which is likely to stir up hatred against a racial group.

Race Relations in the United States of America

Racial tension in the USA between blacks and whites is linked to the ownership of slaves in the Southern states which began in the 1600s. Slaves were used on the cotton and tobacco plantations because the climate was too hot for the white owners to work in, and there was a shortage of labour. Slaves were brought from Africa and sold to plantation owners. The slaves were regarded as personal property with no rights of their own.

Slavery was abolished in the USA in 1865. However, the blacks did not gain equal rights, since many whites still believed that blacks were an inferior race.

Organisations such as the Ku-Klux-Klan were formed to ensure white supremacy. Whites and blacks were segregated. They had to attend different schools, sit in separate sections of public transport, and eat at different tables in cafés. The blacks were allocated inferior housing and offered fewer employment opportunities.

In the 1960s, the Civil Rights Movement began to protest actively against discrimination. The 'Black Power' movement gained ground and contained several groups which believed that violence was an acceptable means to achieving equal rights. Men such as Malcolm X and Stokely Carmichael advocated the use of violence. However, the man who was most successful in gaining civil rights for the blacks was Martin Luther King, and he believed in a policy of non-violence. King travelled throughout the South organising marches to protest against injustice. He was assassinated in Memphis in 1968, but the Civil Rights Movement has continued to grow and has obtained substantial concessions for the black population of the USA.

Race Relations in South Africa

In South Africa the political system segregrated the different racial groups and was called *apartheid*.

Apartheid divided the population of South Africa into four separate groups: Asian, Black, Coloured, White. The classification given at birth decided the type of work, education, political rights and housing open to a person. The Whites were the privileged group.

The issue of cheap labour was crucial to the policy of apartheid. By keeping the black population poorly paid, segregated and without power, the white minority prevented the blacks from becoming powerful.

Several methods were used to keep the black population in an inferior position:

- **Homelands.** The African population was settled into the Homelands called Bantustans. In order to leave the Homelands, an African had to obtain a pass.
- **The Pass Laws.** The Pass Laws required black South Africans to carry a pass at all times when out of the Bantustans. Passes were granted only to workers.
- **Low pay.** The Africans are the lowest-paid sector of South African society. The whites have a comfortable standard of living. Most blacks live only a little above subsistence level.
- **Education.** The education system was segregated. There was a shortage of school places for blacks, and few Africans went on to higher education.
- **Political representation.** At the present time, political power and control of the state is still in the hands of those classified as White.

- **Censorship.** There was no freedom of information. Material intended as a protest at the system, or that might cause civil unrest, was banned. In recent years, much of the censorship has been relaxed.
- **Militarisation.** The police force and the army are armed, and in the event of rebellion use their weapons without hesitation.

Protest Against Apartheid

Sanctions were taken against South Africa by other countries to try to persuade the Government to change its policies. Many countries did not trade or have sporting links with South Africa for many years.

Within South Africa there was also a growing call for freedom. In March 1960, the police opened fire on a peaceful anti-Pass Law demonstration at Sharpeville, killing 69 people and injuring 180. Organisations have been formed to protest against the various aspects of apartheid. As the protests grew, the Government banned all such organisations, although these continued underground. Some protestors believed in peaceful protest and others believed in violence. Two Christians, Bishop Trevor Huddleston and Bishop Desmond Tutu, believe in a peaceful protest, whereas Nelson and Winnie Mandela supported the use of violence.

When F. W. de Klerk became President, changes began to take place in the political system of South Africa. Nelson Mandela was freed from prison and ANC President Oliver Tambo returned from exile overseas. Sporting links with South Africa were renewed.

As the strict rules of apartheid have been relaxed, violence has gradually grown between rival black groups in the townships, and beatings and killings have become everyday occurrences. Political leaders are resolutely pursuing ways to resolve South Africa's very complex problems. Progress is steady rather than dramatic, but it does seem to be taking place.

Biblical Teaching on Race

Genesis states that people are made in God's image and all are descended from Adam and Eve. Therefore, all people must be one race, and members of the same family. If all are equal in God's sight, then prejudice is a sin. Jesus was willing to mix with anyone, whatever their political, social or religious status, and he taught that prejudice is wrong.

The Samaritan Village (Luke 9,51-56)

When Jesus was rejected by a Samaritan village, his followers wanted to destroy that village. Jesus told them that they must not behave in this way. They must take another route. Jesus was teaching that if Christians experience prejudice, they must not retaliate but must walk away.

The Parable of the Great Feast (Luke 14,15-24)

Here, Jesus teaches that God accepts all races, and in many ways it is the other races who behave better than the Jews, as they will accept his message that everyone is welcomed into God's kingdom. Those who reject this fact will have to remain outside the kingdom.

The Centurion's Servant (Luke 7,1-10)

In Jesus's time, the Romans were the most hated group of Gentiles because they were the occupying army. Romans worshipped many gods, but this incident shows that even though the centurion was of a different race and religion from the Jews, he could still understand how important their beliefs were to them. In fact, the centurion had built a synagogue for the Jews, and as a result the Jews respected him and wanted to help him when his servant was ill.

The incident shows that two races are able to live in peace side by side, respecting one another's way of life and helping each other in times of trouble.

The Conversion of Cornelius (Acts 11,1-18)

At first, the followers of Jesus believed that Christianity was only for Jews, and that any Gentile wishing to become a Christian would first have to convert to Judaism. But Peter had a vision which made him realise that Christianity was for everyone. Immediately after this dream, he was asked to go to the home of a Roman centurion, Cornelius. Cornelius was the first Gentile convert to be admitted to Christianity. This story demonstrates that God regards everyone as equal.

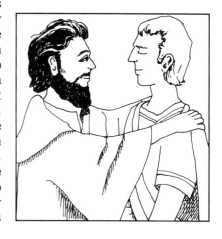

All Christians are Equal (Galatians 3,26-28)

Paul taught that when a person is baptised as a Christian, race, class and sex cease to matter. Christians become one in Christ.

13 The Distribution of Wealth in the World

Developing Countries

The poor countries of the world are known as the developing countries (the 'South') and include most countries in South America, Africa and Asia. The rich countries are known as developed countries (the 'North') and include North America, Europe, Russia, Japan and Australasia.

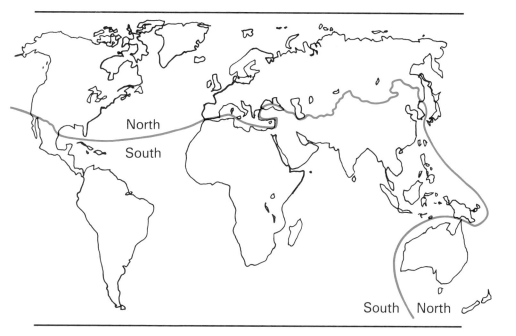

There is sufficient wealth in the world to meet the needs of the world's population, but the distribution of this wealth is unequal. One quarter of the world's population lives in the developed 'North' and has at its disposal four-fifths of the world's wealth. This means that the people of the 'North' can expect a longer life, better education and a higher standard of living than the people of the developing 'South'.

Biblical teaching on wealth is particularly relevant to the needs of the developing countries. It is not true that there is insufficient food in the world, but rather, that the rich countries ignore the needs of the poor countries. Christians must work to change these attitudes and to help those in poverty to achieve a higher standard of living.

Attitudes Towards Problems of the Developing Countries

The Brandt Report stated that the developed countries not only have a duty to help the developing countries, but that it is also in their own best interests to do so, since if the developing countries grow poorer, the 'South' will be forced to reduce the number of manufactured goods it purchases from the 'North', and as a result the wealth of the developed countries will decline.

The help given to developing countries should not only consist of emergency aid, but should also include funds to set up projects which will help overcome the long-term results of poverty such as malnutrition, illiteracy and disease.

The Major Problems of the Developing Countries

The four major problems experienced by the developing countries are poverty, hunger, disease and population explosion.

Poverty

The developing countries have only one-fifth of the world's income to share between three-quarters of the world's population.

Poverty is a vicious circle since it means that there is no money available to provide the improvements in education, medical care, farming methods and industry which would help to reduce poverty.

Poverty in the developing countries could be eased in the following ways:

● Industry and money used for arms production could instead be used to improve the standard of living in developing countries;

● A World Development Fund could be set up to distribute resources to the countries in need of financial help;

● Banks in the 'North' provide loans to the poorer countries at reduced interest rates;

● Developed countries prefer to import commodities in their raw state because there is less duty to pay. If developing countries had a share in the processing, marketing, transport and distribution of products made from their own raw materials, their domestic industries would earn more.

Hunger

There are two forms of hunger in the developing countries:

1. Starvation – when there is not enough for people to eat;

2. Malnutrition – when there is sufficient food, but it does not provide a balanced diet.

In developing countries, many different factors can cause hunger, for example:

● A shortage of water means that crops cannot be irrigated, so they fail through drought.

- Floods destroy crops – for example, Bangladesh is particularly prone to flooding.
- The people lack knowledge of farming methods, such as the use of fertilisers, which would increase the yield from their land.
- Many of the plants and animals suffer from diseases or pests which cause wasting and death.
- Transportation of food between areas is difficult.
- Food storage is a problem in hot climates. Enough food may be produced, but it cannot be stored long enough to be available in times of shortage.
- 'Cash crops' such as rice, which could help to feed the local population, are sold abroad because a better price can be obtained.
- Few countries use their natural resources, such as fish, to feed their population.

Possible long-term solutions to the problems of hunger in the developing countries include the following:

- Teach new farming methods in order to improve the yield from the land.
- Carry out research to produce pesticides and find cures for the diseases which affect the plants and animals.
- Find new sources of food – for example, in recent years the soya bean has provided a new source of protein.
- Encourage people to use natural resources of food, such as fish.
- Improve the transportation and storage of food, so that everyone has access to food at all times.

Disease

People in developing countries have less access to medical care than people in the 'North'. The death rate for children under four is 20% higher in underdeveloped countries than it is in Britain. The average life expectancy in these countries is only fifty years.

Many of the diseases of the developing countries are caused by poor diet. If people's nutrition is improved, their health will also improve. Other causes of poor health include:

- Poor sanitation – as a result of this, drinking water becomes contaminated, leading to diseases such as typhoid and river blindness.

● Insect-borne diseases – e.g. malaria from mosquito bites, or sleeping sickness from the tsetse fly.

● Overcrowding – many people live in overcrowded conditions and have poor standards of hygiene, so diseases such as tuberculosis and cholera spread easily.

● Lack of money – medicines have to be imported, and are too expensive for many developing countries to afford.

As well as improving nutrition, other ways of overcoming these problems include:

● Providing basic sanitation so that drinking water is clean, and sewage is disposed of safely;

● Teaching people, especially mothers, the importance of hygiene as a way of improving health;

● Immunising children against killer diseases of the developing world – e.g. measles;

● Controlling insects to prevent the spreading of disease – e.g. by draining swamps or spraying breeding places;

● Setting up training schemes to educate local people to deal with simple medical problems;

● Training more doctors and nurses and building more hospitals to overcome the shortage of skilled medical care.

Population Explosion

The improvements already made in health care and nutrition have had one adverse effect on the developing countries – a population explosion. Despite the fact that more children are surviving to maturity, couples have continued to have large families in order to ensure that some children will survive to provide a labour force, and to care for them in old age. This population explosion is increasing the pressure on the already limited resources of the developing countries. Some suggestions which have been put forward to try to solve these problems are:

● People need to be convinced that large families are no longer necessary. Poster campaigns have been used to explain why smaller families are better.

● Education on the use of contraceptives should be available at local clinics, where free contraceptives are provided.

● If the education and standard of living of people is improved, there seems to be a natural tendency for couples to have fewer children.

Voluntary Work in the Developing Countries

Many organisations are working to try to solve the problems of the developing countries, and to provide long-term aid as well as emergency relief. Most of this work is carried out by voluntary organisations, independent of their Governments.

Most Governments of developed countries allocate part of their budget to pay for aid to the developing countries. Money is also donated to the various branches of the United Nations working in developing countries, e.g. UNICEF. Two organisations in Britain which are working to solve overseas problems are Christian Aid and OXFAM, which is not affiliated to any religious group.

The Christian Attitude to Wealth

The teaching of Jesus is not against the possession of wealth. However, those with wealth have a duty to use it for the good of those in need. The rich must not be blinded by their wealth to the poverty of others.

A Christian should not be working for material possessions in this world, but for eternal rewards in heaven. In the Sermon on the Mount, Jesus warns that a person cannot serve two masters – money and God. A choice must be made between the two, and for a Christian that choice must be God.

Naboth's Vineyard (I Kings 21,1-19)

This incident is a warning against greed. King Ahab sees a vineyard that he wants. Queen Jezebel uses the king's power to accuse Naboth falsely, causing his death, whereupon Ahab takes possession of the vineyard. The prophet Elijah tells King Ahab that as a result of this misuse of power and position, disaster will fall upon the King and his family.

The Parable of the Rich Man and Lazarus (Luke 16,19-31)

The rich man finds himself in Hell, not because he lived in comfort but because he failed to notice the beggar, Lazarus, and to feed him. The rich man is reminded that in the Old Testament there are warnings that such selfishness would be punished, so he has no excuse for his neglect of Lazarus.

The Parable of the Rich Fool (Luke 12,13-21)

This parable teaches the dangers of the pursuit of wealth. A farmer puts all his efforts into getting rich, and when he thinks he can retire and enjoy his wealth, he dies. All his possessions are inherited by someone who has not worked for them, and the rich man has done nothing which is of value in God's eyes.

The Parable of the Sheep and the Goats (Matthew 25,31-46)

This parable describes those who will be rewarded by God on the Day of Judgement, and those who will be punished. The people who will be given eternal life are those who have followed the teaching of Jesus by helping people in need. Those who disregarded Jesus's teaching by ignoring the needy will go to Hell.

Barnabas and the Community Life of the Church (Acts 4,32-37)

If those who have wealth share it with the poor, there will be enough for everyone and there will be no hunger or poverty. The early Church put this into practice by all members sharing their possessions.

Barnabas sold the field he owned so that every member of the community could have an equal share of his wealth.

A Brother in Need (I John 3,17-18)

John warns that if a rich person ignores those in need, he is also closing his heart to God. A true believer not only speaks about loving his neighbour, but acts in such a way that he demonstrates love of his neighbour.

14 | War, Peace and the Use of Force

War

A war is an armed conflict. It can be defined as an outbreak of violence involving the use of armed forces by at least one side.

Causes of War

No two wars have exactly the same cause, but there are similar 'roots' to wars.

● When an individual or a nation wishes to be more powerful, other nations are attacked.

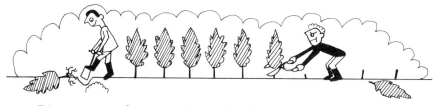

● Disputes over the ownership of land can result in war.
● Disagreement over the political system adopted by a country can lead to conflict.
● A country seeking independence from another country may resort to war to gain its freedom.
● Differences over religious beliefs can cause conflict.
● When attacked by another group or nation, a country has to defend itself.

Types of War

A war may take one of several different forms.

● **A conventional war** is fought when large armies face each other in battle. The armies use conventional weapons such as guns and tanks.
● **A civil war** is a war in which people from the same nation fight each other within that country.
● **Guerrilla warfare** takes place when an unofficial army fights a strong, well-equipped force. The guerrillas use 'hit-and-run' tactics against the enemy. Guerrillas have to use whatever weapons are available, and these usually consist of hand-guns and home-made bombs.
● **Terrorism** exists when a group believes itself to be at war with a political system. As a result of this, everyone involved in that system is

seen as an enemy. To try to change the system, and to gain publicity for their cause, terrorists use violence, such as bombing and shooting.

- **Chemical and biological warfare** are outlawed by most countries. Chemical warfare uses chemicals such as nerve gas to defeat an enemy, whereas biological warfare involves the use of germs to disable an enemy.
- **Nuclear war** makes use of nuclear weapons. This form of war involves directing nuclear missiles, or atomic bombs, at an enemy.

A Holy War

A holy war is fought by people who believe that they have God on their side – that is, they believe their cause is right. The war is fought for God, and therefore the spoils of war belong to God.

The Battle of Jericho (Joshua 6,15-21; 7,15-26) is an example of a holy war because:

- The Hebrews believed they were God's chosen people and therefore must fight for His cause.
- God had demonstrated that He was protecting the Hebrews by the miracles He had performed to help their cause, and God had spoken to their leader, Joshua.
- Canaan was the Promised Land given to the Hebrews by God, and they believed they were justified in trying to win the land back.
- The Hebrews had to prove to the Canaanites that Yahweh was the only God and that the idols worshipped in Jericho had no power.

The biblical account of the Battle of Jericho ends with the story of Achan's sin. Achan disobeyed God when he stole some of the treasure from Jericho, and as a result the Hebrews lost their next battle. When the theft was discovered, Achan and his family were executed on God's orders.

This incident teaches that in a holy war God must be obeyed, and that all the spoils of war belong to God. Those who disobey God will bring disaster on themselves, their family and their friends.

The 'Just' War

Another belief about war is that there are times when wars *have* to be fought. These wars, called 'just' wars, must follow rules if they are to be morally right (just). Many Christians agree with and support the concept of the just war.

St Thomas Aquinas laid down the following conditions for a just war:

- The war must only be started and controlled by the Government of the nation going to war.
- There must be a just cause for the war – for example, the nation has been attacked and has to fight in order to defend itself.
- The war must be fought to promote good or to avoid evil, and peace and justice must be restored as soon as possible.

Two other conditions have been added to the concept of what makes a war just:

- War must be the last resort, after all other methods to solve the problem have been tried and have failed.
- Innocent civilians, such as the young, the old and the sick, must not be harmed by the fighting.

Pacifism

Many people believe that however 'just' the cause, war is not the solution. Violence, they believe, is a short-term solution. It is better to sit down and discuss differences rather than to go to war.

Pacifists are people who refuse to fight under any circumstances. They promote the idea that war and violence should be abolished.

Conscientious objectors are pacifists who refuse to fight in a war because their conscience does not allow it.

Many pacifists have performed brave deeds during wartime, such as acting as stretcher-bearers and ambulance drivers on the front line. Members of the Society of Friends (Quakers) are pacifists because they believe that violence goes against the teaching of Jesus to 'love thy neighbour'.

Arguments in Favour of Pacifism

- When people are attacked, they respond with violence. It is only by refusing to fight that this spiral of violence may be stopped.
- A Christian should not be violent, because violence goes against all aspects of Jesus's teaching.
- Violence is wasteful because of:
    a) the loss of life or injury to soldiers and civilians;
    b) the cost to a country of the war itself, and the cost of replacing property and industry, and paying pensions to the injured and to war widows;
    c) the many people who are left stateless after a war and who have to be supported by other nations.

Arguments Against Pacifism

- Jesus, aware that wars would happen, said, 'no greater love has a man than to lay down his life for a friend'.
- Jesus talked of establishing God's kingdom in this world. If this is

to happen, Christians will have to fight evil.

- Jesus taught people to 'love your neighbour'. It is not loving to ignore a 'neighbour' who is being attacked.
- If your country is fighting to survive, it is selfish to expect to be defended without taking part in the fighting yourself.

Disarmament

Disarmament is the getting rid of weapons of war. Nuclear disarmament is the getting rid of nuclear weapons.

People disagree about whether nuclear disarmament is wise. The Campaign for Nuclear Disarmament (CND) wants Britain to get rid of its nuclear weapons, whereas the North Atlantic Treaty Organisation (NATO) believes Britain should keep them.

Unilateral disarmament arises when one country decides to give up its weapons in the hope that other nations will follow its example.

Multilateral disarmament occurs when several countries agree to give up their weapons.

Arguments in Favour of Nuclear Disarmament

- It is morally wrong to threaten to use a weapon which could result in *genocide* (the complete destruction of a race or nation).
- A country which possesses nuclear weapons would be a prime target if war did break out.
- The huge cost of producing nuclear weapons, which are unlikely to be used, would be better employed in solving the world's problems.
- A nuclear weapon could be launched in error. Too great a risk!
- Nuclear weapons could fall into the hands of terrorists, who could then hold the world to ransom.
- The effects of a nuclear war would be felt for centuries. It is wrong to inflict such a future on our descendants.
- If a conventional war breaks out between nations, it could escalate to the point where nuclear weapons are used. If nuclear weapons are no longer available, this risk is removed.

Arguments Against Nuclear Disarmament

- Nuclear weapons prevent wars by acting as a deterrent. The countries involved in conflict are fearful of a nuclear attack, and so settle their disagreements peacefully.
- If one country gives up its weapons, it is open to attack from stronger nations. Countries must keep nuclear weapons in order to protect themselves.
- The manufacture of nuclear weapons is a major industry. To cease production would cause considerable unemployment.

Biblical Teaching on War

In the Old Testament there are many battles. However, Genesis makes it clear that this is not what God intended for mankind, and that violence is the result of Man's disobedience in the Garden of Eden. Many of the prophets of the Old Testament teach that war is God's punishment on those who disobey his commandments. If God is obeyed, a time of peace will come. The weapons of war will no longer be needed and the metal they are made from may be put to a peaceful use. The prophets Micah and Isaiah both speak of a time when swords will be turned into 'pruning-forks and ploughshares'.

In the New Testament, Jesus taught that Christians must forgive their enemies, not fight them.

The Temptation of Jesus (Matthew 4,1-11)

When tempted by the Devil to accept power in this world, Jesus refused. Worldly power lasts only a lifetime, whereas the kingdom which Jesus offers is eternal, and with God.

Loving Our Enemies
(Matthew 5,38-48)

In the Sermon on the Mount, Jesus teaches that revenge is wrong and that we must love our enemies. If a Christian is wronged, he or she must not seek revenge, but instead must turn away from violent action. A Christian must do everything possible to keep the peace.

The Arrest of Jesus (Matthew 26,47-53)

When Jesus was arrested, by his words and actions he showed that whatever the provocation, and however dangerous the situation, violence is not the answer. Violence only makes matters worse – it leads to further violence, and death.

The Authority of the State (Romans 13,1-7)

Paul wrote that the authority of the state is placed there by God and must be obeyed. Christians must avoid civil disobedience, as to challenge the existing authority is to oppose God's order. It is the duty of state authorities to serve God and do good in the land. Christians who reject this principle of government will be punished by God.

SECTION 3: Aspects of Christian Life with Reference to the Roman Catholic Tradition

Introduction

Sacraments are central to the lives of Roman Catholics. These symbolic acts enable Catholics to meet Christ in special ways. Catholics believe that Christ influences them in the most decisive moments of their lives through the sacraments

This section covers the seven sacraments of the Roman Catholic Church, and for each of the sacraments the following aspects are studied:

Rite or Ceremony;
Meaning and Symbolism;
Related Issues.

.5 Baptism

Baptism is the first sacrament any Roman Catholic receives. Jesus showed his acceptance of baptism when he was baptised in the River Jordan by John, and when he instructed his apostles to baptise people.

The Rite or Ceremony of Baptism

Prior to the ceremony, parents and godparents have been prepared, perhaps by attending classes, to learn about their responsibilities as they make promises on behalf of the child. At the ceremony, the family of the child are present together with members of the Church community into which the child is being welcomed.

The Baptism may be celebrated during Mass, ideally at Easter, but is often celebrated as an individual sacrament. More than one child may be baptised at the same time.

Reception

The priest welcomes the family and asks the child's name. The child is signed with the sign of the cross on the forehead and welcomed into the Christian community. The sign of the cross signifies that the child now belongs to God.

Celebration of God's Word

This includes readings and bidding prayers (prayers of intercession) to prepare everyone involved in the ceremony.

Exorcism and Anointing

The child is *exorcised* (evil is expelled) and anointed with the oil of catechumens on the breast to strengthen him or her with the power of Christ. Anointing is a sign of strength and healing.

Celebration of the Sacrament

- The priest blesses the water.
- The parents and godparents are asked to renew their baptismal

95

promises in order to signify their intention of bringing up the child in the faith.

• Actual baptism – the priest pours water over the child's head and says, '(child's name), I baptise you in the name of the Father and of the Son and of the Holy Spirit.'

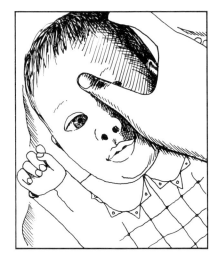

• The child is anointed with *chrism* (perfumed oil) to consecrate him or her to God. This is a sign that the child is being appointed to do very important work.

• The white garment is put on the child as an outward sign of his or her new Christian dignity and purity.

• A candle is given to one of the parents, who lights it from the Paschal candle. This symbolises the child receiving the light of Christ.

Conclusion

Everyone says the Lord's Prayer and the priest blesses the mother, the father and all the congregation.

Meaning and Symbolism

Four aspects of the sacrament of Baptism may be distinguished.

1. Initiation

Baptism is an initiation ceremony which makes people members of the Christian community. Christians become members of the Body of Christ and begin to share in the privileges of life within the community. This is shown in the rite at the reception and with the sign of the cross.

2. New Life

Baptism gives new life in Christ. 'Baptism' means immersion. In Jesus's day, when people were fully immersed under water, baptism was thought of as 'plunging into death' (drowning) and arising with a new life. Today, we use the sign of pouring water for convenience. Catholics receive Christ's love and grace to guide them in their new life. This is shown in the rite with the symbolism of water, white garment and candle, at the exorcism, giving of the Christian name, and in the baptismal promises.

3. Power

Baptism gives the power to worship. Christians receive God's love and are empowered to return it. It confers the character of Christ. It is permanent and unchangeable – a person can be baptised only once. No other sacrament can be received unless baptism has taken place. This is shown in the rite at the anointing and with the symbolism of the white garment and the lighted candle.

4. Salvation

A person should be baptised before he or she can be saved (i.e. go to heaven). The child is cleansed of original sin and all actual sin committed prior to baptism. It is the parents' responsibility to have their child baptised and to train the child in the faith. Catholics believe that any who refuse baptism expose themselves to the danger of eternal damnation. For this reason, anyone may baptise another in an emergency (when a person is in danger of death) – even non-Christians. This is shown in the rite at the anointing with chrism.

If there is no possibility of baptism, a person may be saved by baptism by blood or baptism by desire.

Baptism by Blood occurs when someone dies for their faith (martyrdom). They are, in effect, baptised in their own blood.

Baptism by Desire is when a person, living and acting according to his or her conscience, does what is right according to Christian teaching, even though the person may not be aware of his or her conformity.

Related Issues

Baptism celebrates the gift of human life from God.

Two issues may put the sanctity of human life at risk: contraception and abortion (see also Chapter 11: Decisions of Life and Living).

Contraception

Contraception refers to the various methods which couples use to try to avoid unwanted pregnancies. Responsible couples normally wish to plan families. There are two main methods of family planning:

1. natural methods;
2. artificial methods.

Natural Methods involve avoiding intercourse at the times when a woman is fertile for a few days of her menstrual cycle. This is the only method in accordance with the teaching of the Roman Catholic Church.

Artificial Methods involve taking or using an aid to avoid conception, e.g. the pill, the cap, the condom, or to prevent the fertilised egg from implanting in the womb (an early abortion), e.g. the mini-pill, the 'morning-after' pill, the coil.

Artificial methods are not acceptable to Roman Catholics because:
- they interfere with the Creator's design;
- they involve only one of the couple in taking responsibility;
- they may be harmful, either physically or psychologically;
- they can encourage promiscuity.

Roman Catholics should try to practise the use of natural methods of contraception. In certain difficult circumstances, however, artificial methods may be considered, but it must be realised that this is falling short of the ideal and should be avoided if possible. The Church is concerned that sterilisation and artificial methods of contraception should not be imposed by the State in order to control population.

Abortion

Abortion is the ending of a pregnancy before birth, either by natural means (miscarriage) or by an operation to cause it (procured or induced abortion). The term 'abortion' is usually understood to refer to a procured abortion. Some abortions are performed within the National Health Service; others are paid for privately.

The Abortion Act of 1967 allowed abortions up to the 28th week of pregnancy with the consent of two registered doctors in two instances:

1. If the mother would be physically or psychologically damaged by going through with the pregnancy.

2. If there was the risk of a handicapped child being born.

The law was devised at a time when it was considered that a child could survive outside the womb at 28 weeks of pregnancy but not before. There have been a number of scientific advances since then, and nowadays babies as young as 21 weeks can survive with special care. Because of this, many people believe that the law should be changed. Currently, the limit for legal abortions is restricted to 24 weeks. Abortion is allowed up to birth where the baby may be handicapped or if there would be severe risk to the mother's life if she goes ahead with the pregnancy.

Many people support the right of a woman to have an abortion, including some of the Protestant Churches.

There is much argument about the circumstances in which abortion should be allowed. Arguments used by those in favour of abortion include:

1. Life begins when the baby can live outside its mother's womb.

2. A woman has the right to choose what to do with her own body.

Such situations may include:
- If the child is likely to be handicapped.
- If the mother is under 16 or unmarried.
- If the pregnancy is the result of rape.
- If financial hardship would ensue if the baby were born.

In its document 'The Declaration on Procured Abortion', published in 1974, the Roman Catholic Church teaches that abortion is never acceptable in any circumstances, except when both the mother *and* the baby will die if the pregnancy continues (then the abortion becomes an operation to save life, rather than to take it).

The teaching is based on the belief that all life is sacred – it is a gift from God and no one has the right to take life except God. Life begins at the moment of conception and everyone has a right to life. The mother has no more rights than the foetus in her womb, so Roman Catholics consider abortion to be murder.

The Roman Catholic Church teaches that abortion is wrong, though Catholics should not condemn women who have abortions, but should be actively involved in offering practical help and in changing the law. Two anti-abortion groups are SPUC (Society for the Protection of the Unborn Child), and Life. Not all members are Catholics.

16 Marriage

The sacrament of marriage in the Roman Catholic Church is a solemn and holy contract between a man and a woman who love each other.

The Rite or Ceremony of Marriage

Prior to the ceremony the couple will usually have been prepared, perhaps by attending classes, so that they fully understand the vows they are undertaking. At the ceremony, the family and friends of the couple, together with members of the Church community and the priest, are present to witness the marriage. The marriage may be celebrated during Mass (Nuptial Mass) if the couple wish. (The exchange of vows and rings occurs after the readings and before the Liturgy of the Eucharist is celebrated, and the nuptial blessing is said after the Lord's Prayer.) The rite for celebrating marriage outside Mass is as follows:

Welcome

Usually the bride progresses to the altar where she meets her groom. The priest greets the couple and all the congregation.

Liturgy of the Word

This includes bible readings and a *homily* (sermon) by the priest to prepare everyone involved in the ceremony.

Celebration of the Sacrament

● The priest questions the couple individually to ensure they fully understand their responsibilities in marriage. They are asked about their freedom of choice, faithfulness to each other, and the acceptance and upbringing of children.

● The couple make vows to each other. They join hands (the bride's father may 'give his daughter away' by placing her hand in the groom's hand) and say individually, in these or similar words: 'I .... take you .... to be my lawful wedded wife/husband; to have and to hold from this day forward, for better, for worse, for richer, for poorer, in sickness and in health, to love and to cherish, till death do us part.'

- The priest, who represents the Church, accepts the agreement the couple have made and asks God to bless them.
- Rings are blessed and exchanged. The ring is a sign of the couple's everlasting love and faithfulness to each other in their marriage.

Prayers of the Faithful

Bidding prayers are offered for the needs of the newly married couple.

The Nuptial Blessing

The priest says a special blessing over the couple in which he expresses the meaning of the sacrament.

Register

This is completed to fulfil civil requirements. The priest may be an authorised registrar but, if not, a registrar must be present to witness the signing of the register.

The sacrament is completed once the marriage has been *consummated* (sexual relations have taken place).

Meaning and Symbolism

A Christian marriage is a living sign of God's love, reflected in the love the couple have for each other. It is a calling from God to help one another become loving and holy people. A married couple is a symbol of the Church. St. Paul compared the love a man has for his wife with the love of Christ for his Church.

Christian marriage is also a *covenant* (an agreement or a promise) to give unconditional love. The ministers of the sacrament are the couple themselves. The sacrament is received the moment the vows are exchanged. The man and woman make the love of Christ present to each other and this continues especially in their sexual relationship. The priest is the Church's official witness to the sacrament.

The teaching of the Church on the meaning of the sacrament of marriage is expressed in the Pope's letter 'Humanae Vitae', which was circulated in 1968. In this, four characteristic features of married love can be distinguished:

1. Marriage is Fully Human

We are formed by our relationships with others and become more human.

2. Marriage is Total

Marriage is a total giving of self as expressed uniquely in the sex-act. It means to love a person for his or her own sake, rather than for what you can get out of a relationship.

3. Marriage is Faithful

Married love is faithful and exclusive of all others until death.

4. Marriage is Fruitful

Married love deepens between husband and wife and is life-giving in their sexual relationship. In sexual intercourse, man and woman share most intimately in God's creative love and can create life itself through God's love.

The Roman Catholic Church teaches that each and every act of sexual intercourse must remain open to the transmission of life. Parents have a responsibility to love, care for and educate their children in the Catholic faith (Colossians 3,18-21).

The signs of the vows, the exchange of rings, and the blessing within the ceremony itself, all show the meaning of a Catholic marriage.

Related Issues

There are three main issues which may cause problems in relationships: sex outside marriage, marital breakdown, and family planning. The Roman Catholic Church provides guidelines on these issues, based on the teaching of Jesus (see also Chapter 11: Decisions of Life and Living).

Sex Outside Marriage

Sex outside marriage may occur in one of two ways:
1. Fornication;
2. Adultery.

Fornication is a sexual relationship between a couple, neither of whom is married. The Church teaches that sexual intercourse should occur only within a marriage relationship. The giving of oneself in sex is such a precious intimate act (the couple making love are making Christ present to each other) that the sex act should not be demeaned by occurring outside the sacrament of marriage. The relationship may break down, leaving one or both partners feeling used and resentful. Also, the sex act should be life-giving. The Church teaches that responsible parenthood involves bringing up children in a happy, stable, married relationship. A sexual relationship before marriage can lead to great unhappiness, and it is because the Church wants people to be happy in their relationships with each other, and with God, that it teaches that sex before marriage is wrong.

St. Paul teaches (1 Corinthians 6,18-20) that people should guard against immorality, as our bodies are temples of the Holy Spirit who lives within us. He says that within marriage, sex is very important and is necessary and human (1 Corinthians 7,2-5).

The Church teaches that homosexual behaviour is wrong, that it is a misuse of a person's sexuality. Homosexual relationships can be love-sharing but cannot be life-giving.

Adultery is a sexual relationship between a married person and someone other than his or her partner. The Church teaches that adultery is wrong as it breaks marriage vows. Jesus taught (Matthew 5,27-30) that nothing should be allowed to break the faithful and exclusive bond of married love. He said adultery is wrong, but also suggested that even to think adulterous thoughts was wrong because it could lead to adultery. However, Jesus also taught that we should not condemn those who have sinned in this way, and he forgave the adulterous woman (John 8,1-11).

Marital Breakdown

The couple in the sacrament of marriage make a lifetime commitment and the marriage vows cannot be broken, as Christ's vows to the Church can never be broken. There are many pressures on marital relationships, particularly in these times, which can lead to enormous unhappiness and irretrievable breakdown. The Roman Catholic Church recognises that these pressures exist, but suggests that every effort should be made by the couple and the Catholic community to rekindle the loving marriage relationship. In some cases, it is  accepted that this may not be possible and that it is advisable for the couple to separate, even to seek a legal divorce in extreme circumstances. However, in the eyes of the Church, the couple remain married to each other for life and so they cannot marry other partners.

According to the law, they can remarry in a civil ceremony, but it is not a sacramental marriage and would be seen by the Church as adultery. Jesus taught (Matthew 5,31-32) that remarriage was committing adultery and St. Paul underlines this (1 Corinthians 7,10-11) by saying divorce is unacceptable.

In some cases where a marriage relationship has broken down, a very special sort of enquiry into the marriage is carried out by the Church authorities, after which an *annulment* may be granted. A marriage may be annulled (declared invalid) when it is considered that the sacrament of marriage never actually occurred: the vows were never intended, and so were not valid, or the marriage was not consummated. Each case is looked at individually and there are no easy rules and regulations for the granting of annulment. However, an example might be if one of the couple never intended to have children, or if the couple were pressurised into getting married by others and were not making the commitment of their own free will. Annulment is not the same as divorce, which is when vows are broken. In an annulment, the vows are regarded as never having been made or completed.

In general, a divorced man or woman, or a person who has married a divorced person (whose marriage is therefore not sacramentally valid) cannot receive the sacraments, but special permission can be given so that a person may receive Holy Communion. The Church community should respond with loving forgiveness to people who have broken relationships, as Jesus did to the adulterous woman.

Family Planning

The Catholic Church encourages responsible parenthood and advises that natural methods of family planning are best (see section on Contraception under Baptism: Related Issues, page 97).

7 Confirmation

Confirmation is one of the three sacraments of initiation into the Roman Catholic Church, the other two being Baptism and Eucharist. Confirmation is usually celebrated when a person is old enough to make his or her own personal commitment to the sacrament (13 +), but can be celebrated at any age. There is much discussion in the Church about the age at which Confirmation should be celebrated.

Preparation for Confirmation

Confirmation preparation programmes are very important so that the candidate fully understands what he or she is accepting in affirming his or her faith.

A typical preparation programme may include instruction at school and attendance at small group sessions in the parish with a catechist, a reconciliation service, a retreat, celebration of Mass, and the completion of a confirmation card including information about baptism, the confirmation name and the sponsor's name.

The Rite or Ceremony of Confirmation

Confirmation is usually administered by the bishop (or in special circumstances by a priest delegated by the bishop) and is celebrated with family members and parish representatives present. The candidates' sponsors play an important role (a sponsor may be a godparent, a teacher, or a friend who can offer support to the candidate). Confirmation is usually celebrated within Mass, between the Liturgy of the Word and the Liturgy of the Eucharist. In the Mass, there are appropriate readings and special bidding prayers.

Presentation of the Candidate

If numbers allow, the candidates are presented individually to the bishop who welcomes them and they are accompanied by their sponsors.

Renewal of Baptismal Promises

The bishop asks the candidates the same questions which were asked at their baptism, so that they themselves now proclaim their beliefs. Unless candidates accept their baptism, they cannot be ready to confirm their faith.

Laying-on of Hands

The bishop extends his hands over the candidates, asking God to send his Holy Spirit.

The Naming and Anointing with Chrism

The candidate kneels or stands before the bishop with the sponsor's right hand on his or her shoulder. The confirmation card is given to the priest, who reads out the confirmation name. The bishop lays his hand on the candidate's head and anoints the forehead in the sign of the cross with the oil of chrism with the words:

'(name) be sealed with the gift of the Holy Spirit'. The candidate responds 'Amen'.

The bishop then gives the sign of peace.

The Final Blessing

The Mass continues as usual, ending with a special blessing.

Meaning and Symbolism

The first-ever confirmation occurred when the apostles received the power and strength of the Holy Spirit at Pentecost (Acts 2,1-4). This story tells how the frightened apostles, in hiding after the death of Jesus, were transformed when visited by the Holy Spirit, after which they were able to go out and preach to all nations. The signs of the Holy Spirit's presence were the wind and tongues of fire which show the strength and power the apostles received.

There are three themes which help us understand the meaning of the sacrament.

1. Initiation

Confirmation is a deeper initiation into the faith community. It is very closely linked to Baptism and at one time the two sacraments were celebrated together. In Baptism, a person becomes a member of the Christian Community and receives God's love. In Confirmation, the person is given the fullness of the Holy Spirit and is sealed in his or her faith. He or she is 'sealed for Mission' and enabled to share his/her faith with others. In the ceremony, the anointing with chrism seals the relationship of God with the candidate. The sign of the cross is like

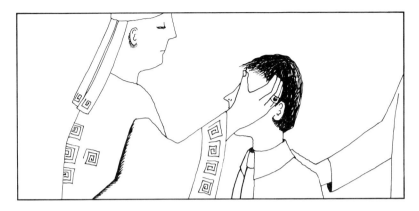

Christ's mark of ownership on us: his signature. The perfume shows the loving relationship of God with his people.

2. Celebration

Confirmation celebrates the gifts of the Holy Spirit which are received in the sacrament. The laying-on of hands illustrates the passing-on of the power and strength of the Holy Spirit, and the prayer said when the bishop does this, describes the seven gifts received: wisdom, understanding, right judgement, knowledge, reverence, courage, and the spirit of wonder and awe. The sign of peace is a reminder of the peace the Holy Spirit brings to the world. All these gifts help the candidate to fulfil the third theme.

3. Witness

Confirmation is a sacrament of witness. Jesus gave his Spirit to help Christians live their lives as true witnesses to their faith, proclaiming his good news and living out their vocation. The laying-on of hands gives Christians the power to do this and the anointing with chrism is a sign that the confirmed person is being appointed to do God's work in the world (in the Old Testament, royalty, priests and prophets were anointed to do special tasks). The confirmation name of a saint is chosen as a sign that the candidate has a new task to carry out in the world.

Related Issues

The issues relate to how confirmation is lived out in the lives of those who have been confirmed. The meanings of vocation, lay ministries and religious congregations need to be considered.

Vocation

Vocation means 'calling'. St. Paul tells us we are God's temple in which the Holy Spirit lives (1 Corinthians 3,16-17). Christ has a special task for all Christians who have a responsibility to fulfil their vocation, to do what Christ wants us to do in the world. The parable of the talents told by Jesus explains how Christians should use the gifts God has given them and how on the last day, they will be judged in Heaven on how they have responded to God's call (Matthew 25,14-30).

Roman Catholics may be called in one of three ways:

1. As a single or married lay person (the laity are baptised people who are full members of the Roman Catholic Church).

2. As a sister or brother in a religious congregation or as a consecrated virgin.

3. As a deacon, priest or bishop (see Sacrament of Holy Orders, page 110).

Lay Ministries

At baptism, Christians are called to holiness 'to be perfect as our Heavenly Father is perfect'. Lay people are called to the priesthood, the *Royal Priesthood*, and share in the mission of Jesus as Priest, Prophet and King. Lay people's vocation or ministry is:

● to preach the word of God (for example, by reading in Church, by being a catechist, as a missionary or by teaching);

● to pray, to strengthen their relationship with God in order to enable them to fulfil their vocation to love God and their neighbour;

● to live their lives by the principles Christ taught and to use the gifts and talents they have. They have a duty to act responsibly in the world and to bear witness to their faith – for example, by serving the parish through taking an active role in Mass or in one of the parish groups such as the S.V.P. (Society of St. Vincent de Paul, which helps the sick and elderly), by running a youth club, or by offering love and support to all those in need, sharing their problems, etc.

The laity must not feel they are good Roman Catholics simply because they attend Sunday Mass; rather, their whole lives should reflect Christ's teaching about loving God and one's neighbour.

Religious Congregations

Jesus called his disciples to leave everything behind (family and possessions) and follow him (Luke 5,1-11, 27-32). They were prepared to make this commitment, unlike the rich young man (Matthew 19,16-30), who was following the commandments but was not prepared to sell all his possessions and give the money to the poor and follow Jesus. The young man refused the call, as all people have a right to do. Jesus warned him about the danger of becoming attached to money and material possessions. It is riches in Heaven which Christians should attempt to gain.

A person receives a call from God to become a *religious* (someone bound by monastic vows). He or she then enquires about the life, and prays and reflects on the call before responding directly to it. It takes many years of prayer and preparation before religious are ready to make their final profession, or vows.

Christians who are called to this special discipleship may choose to belong to either a *contemplative* or an *apostolic* order.

Contemplative nuns or monks live in enclosed orders and do not mix at all with other people. They spend their lives in prayer and work in their own community. Examples are Carmelite or Poor Clare nuns, Carthusian or Cistercian monks.

Apostolic sisters and brothers live in houses among the rest of society, spending their lives in prayer and service in the community, such as teaching, social work, nursing, etc. Examples are Sisters of the Cross and Passion, and Christian Brothers.

All contemplative and apostolic religious consecrate themselves to God by making three vows (evangelical counsels).

1. Poverty. All personal possessions are available for the needs of the Church. The religious are not tied down by money or material possessions, and apostolic orders are free to give themselves in service immediately anywhere in the world, as Christ and his apostles did.

2. Chastity. In imitation of Christ, who never married, the religious sacrifices family life to enable him or her to love as Christ loved. He or she resolves to be pure in mind and body, remaining free to serve all God's family.

3. Obedience. Christ was always obedient to the will of his father, and religious listen carefully to the will of God in every situation. They promise obedience to the work of the order to which they belong.

18 Holy Orders

In the Roman Catholic Church, some men are 'called' to serve God's people, to take the sacrament of Holy Orders (be ordained). Women are not allowed to take Holy Orders because Christ and his apostles were men and this example is followed.

When a man receives Holy Orders, it means he is consecrated to a certain position of leadership and service with various responsibilities in a hierarchical Church. In the early Church, there were many of these specific roles, but today only deacon, priest and bishop have survived.

Preparation for Ordination

Before a man can take Holy Orders, the following conditions must be fulfilled:

- He must want to follow Christ totally. This decision begins with a call by the Holy Spirit which can be freely accepted or rejected.
- He must possess the basic qualities necessary to serve as a deacon, priest, or bishop. For example, he should not be painfully shy and he must have a certain level of intelligence.
- He must be recommended for the priesthood by a bishop or a religious superior.

Once these conditions have been fulfilled, the candidate for the priesthood prepares for the important ministry with many years of study.

The first stage in receiving Holy Orders is when a man is ordained as a deacon (called the *diaconate*). Married men may be ordained deacons, as well as men who are preparing to become priests. Their ministry is guided by a parish priest. *Celibate* (unmarried) men can then go on to be ordained as priests. Few receive the special calling to be bishops.

The Rite or Ceremony of Ordination

Family and friends, priests, and the parish congregation are present to witness the Sacrament of Ordination. This ceremony takes place during Mass and is performed by a bishop. The rites differ for deacons, priests and bishops.

Deacon

After the Liturgy of the Word, the bishop:

1. lays his hands over the candidate's head and says the prayer of ordination;

2. gives him a stole and a *dalmatic* (long, loose garment) to wear as a sign of the diaconate (deacons wear stoles over their left shoulder only);

3. gives him a book of the Gospels so he can preach the word of God.

Mass continues with the Liturgy of the Eucharist.

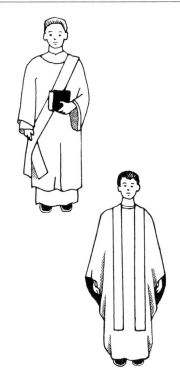

Priest

After the Liturgy of the Word, the Ceremony of Ordination begins.

1. The candidate is presented to the bishop, who gives a homily outlining what the new priest's duties and responsibilities will be.

2. The candidate is questioned by the bishop to ensure that he is prepared to serve God's people. The candidate's hands are placed between the bishop's hands as he promises obedience to him.

3. The congregation pray for the candidate by responding to a litany of saints, while the candidate prostrates himself on the floor as a sign of his total submission to the will of God. A prayer to the Holy Spirit is said.

4. The actual ordination then takes place.

● The bishop lays his hands on the head of the candidate(s), followed by any priests present one by one in silence. A solemn prayer of ordination is said by the bishop.

● The new priest's stole is rearranged to hang loose in front. This is his badge of office. He is also given a *chasuble* (Mass vestment) to wear.

● The priest's hands are anointed with chrism.

● After the offertory procession, the gifts of bread on a *paten* (metal plate) and wine in a *chalice* (goblet) are given to the new priest by the bishop.

● The sign of peace is exchanged between the new priest and the bishop and all the other priests present.

The Mass continues with the Liturgy of the Eucharist, with the new priest consecrating the bread and wine for the very first time.

Bishop

A bishop-elect is ordained by at least three bishops. After the Liturgy of the Word, the presiding bishop gives a sermon and:

1. lays his hands on the head of the bishop-elect;

2. places the Gospel book on the new bishop's head and says the prayer of consecration;

3. anoints the new bishop on the head with chrism and gives him the *mitre* (bishop's hat), the *crozier* (staff), the Gospel book and a ring;

4. leads the new bishop to the *episcopal chair* or *cathedra* (bishop's throne) and gives the sign of peace and a special blessing.

Meaning and Symbolism

The rites of ordination, and the signs and symbols used, illustrate the meaning of the sacrament (which is further discussed in the notes on the Ministry of the Priesthood, page 113).

1. The Laying-on of Hands

This is the most important sign. The bishop passes on the power and strength of the Holy Spirit to the deacon, priest or bishop-elect.

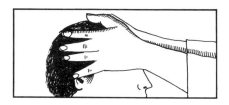

2. The Anointing with Chrism

This is a sign of strength and healing. The priest's hands are anointed to signify the kind of service he will give to God's people. The bishop is anointed on the head as a sign of being appointed to do an important task (as in Confirmation, for example).

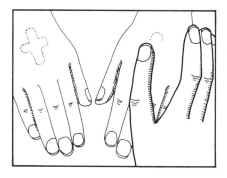

3. The Gifts Received at Ordination

These gifts are signs of the work each man has to do.

- **The deacon receives** a book of the Gospels. He is to preach the word of God. The dalmatic and stole are signs of his diaconate.

- **The priest receives** a paten and chalice. He is to celebrate the Mass. The chasuble and stole are signs of his priesthood. The stole is his badge of office which should always be worn when he celebrates the sacraments.

- **The bishop receives** a mitre, a crozier and an episcopal chair. These are signs that he is successor to the apostles and, like Christ, must be a good shepherd to God's people. The ring shows he is wedded to his *diocese* (area he administrates). The Gospel book shows he is to proclaim the Gospel.

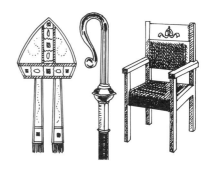

Related Issues

Ministry of the Priesthood

In the ministerial priesthood the different orders or degrees are deacon, priest and bishop. Bishops enjoy the fullness of the sacrament of orders and all priests and deacons look to them for their authority. All share in the priesthood of Jesus Christ who called his apostles to share in his priesthood (Luke 5,1-11,27-32). The twelve apostles responded to his call by leaving everything behind to follow him. The role of deacons, priests and bishops is that of the apostles – to mould the community into a communion of love, to serve the people of God.

The celibacy of priests, bishops and some deacons is a sign which enables them to devote themselves more freely to the service of God and mankind. Many people would argue that married priests could have an important role in the Church, but celibacy is following the model of Jesus who did not marry.

Deacons, priests and bishops serve the community in special ways.

Deacons may read the Gospel at Mass, give the homily, lead public prayers and distribute Holy Communion. They may also baptise, conduct a funeral service and assist at marriages.

Priests act in the person of Christ in three main ways.

- Teach. Their primary duty is to preach the Gospel and explain it.
- Make holy. A priest unites the faithful to God by administering the sacraments, particularly the Eucharist. He continues the saving act of Jesus in the sacrifice of the Mass. In the other sacraments he cares for the sick, reconciles people to God, welcomes new members to the Church, confirms faith and witnesses marriages.
- Govern. Priests share in the office of Christ, leading individuals to a deeper understanding of their own vocation. They assist the bishop, the successor of the apostles, and are obedient to him.

Some priests may not work in a parish but may be teachers, administrators, missionaries, etc.

Bishops proclaim the Gospel and guard the Faith, guide the clergy and act as good shepherds to God's people. Bishops must obey the Pope. Only bishops can administer Holy Orders and they usually perform the sacrament of Confirmation.

19 | The Mass

The sacrament of the Mass is sometimes referred to as Holy Communion or the Eucharist. The Roman Catholic Church teaches that Catholics should attend Mass every Sunday (Resurrection Day), on certain important *feast days* (holy days of obligation), and as often thereafter as is possible. A person should fast for one hour before receiving Holy Communion, to prepare the body to receive Christ. Other Christian groups have communion services, but there are major differences in belief between these and the Catholic Mass.

The Rite or Ceremony of the Mass

Each Mass has a special theme and may be offered for a specific intention (for example, to ask God to heal someone who is sick). It may follow a simple plan or be more elaborate, with many hymns, additional prayers, etc., as appropriate. A simple rite takes the following form:

1. Greeting of the people by the priest and the *penitential rite* (prayers asking God to forgive sins).

2. The Liturgy of the Word (suitable readings, a gospel and a homily or sermon).

3. The Creed (prayer of Catholic belief) and *bidding prayers* (prayers of intercession).

4. The Liturgy of the Eucharist beginning with the preparation of gifts (bread and wine, along with other gifts such as money, are offered to God, sometimes after a procession). The offertory prayer is said.

5. The Eucharistic prayer is said (from a choice of four). It includes the prayer of consecration over the gifts of bread and wine, which transforms them into the Body and Blood of Jesus.

6. The Lord's Prayer is said and the sign of peace is made.

7. Holy Communion/the Eucharist is distributed to those in the congregation able to and wishing to receive it. They receive Christ's body under the appearance of bread and may receive the blood under the appearance of wine.

Special prayers are said before and after communion is given.

8. A blessing and command is given: 'Go in peace to love and serve the Lord.'

Meaning and Symbolism

The Mass is full of symbolism to help illustrate its meaning – for example, bread and wine are the Body and Blood of Jesus; the drop of water the priest puts into the wine represents us drowning in the love of God; the procession of the priest to the altar shows we are a pilgrim people of God.

All the prayers bring out the meaning of the Mass. The readings and homily are like 'food' to the people of God who hear God's teaching to help them live good Christian lives. Hymns help to underline the celebratory aspect of the rite.

Four main themes help to bring out the meaning of the Mass.

1. As a Memorial Meal

At the Last Supper with his disciples (Matthew 26,26-30), Jesus celebrated the Jewish Passover. At the original Passover the Israelites (Jews), who were slaves in Egypt, slaughtered a lamb in sacrifice to Yahweh (God) as he had requested, and smeared the blood on their doorposts. They shared a meal of lamb and unleavened bread (made without yeast because they did not have time to let it rise). The angel of death killed all the first-born of Egypt, but passed over the houses which had been marked. The panic which followed allowed the Israelites to escape from their captors.

Jews celebrate this freedom annually by sharing a special Passover meal. This was the feast Jesus was celebrating with his disciples the night before he died, when he told them to share bread and wine in remembrance of him (Luke 22,19), which Catholics do in the Mass.

2. As a Sacrifice

To sacrifice means 'to make holy'. At the Last Supper, Jesus became the new lamb to be sacrificed. He knew he was going to die, to offer himself as a sacrifice so that people could be saved. A new *covenant* (agreement) was about to be made between God and his people. Just as the bread of the Passover was broken among the disciples, so the body of Jesus would be broken on the cross for the sins of the world. Catholics believe the Mass is a re-enactment of the sacrifice of Christ on the cross.

Through Jesus's sacrifice of himself to his Father, all our sins were forgiven, death was overcome and the gates of Heaven were opened. By offering the sacrifice of the Mass, Jesus's saving action is continued and people are made holy in the love of God.

Catholics believe that the bread and wine are changed into the Body and Blood of Christ in a real, special and mysterious way during Mass (transubstantiation). Through receiving this Body and Blood, Catholics take Christ into themselves and are transformed by his love.

3. As Thanksgiving

Eucharist means 'thanksgiving'. The Mass is a great act of thanksgiving by the people of God for Jesus's sacrifice. Throughout the Mass, God is praised and thanked for the gift of his Son. The gifts of bread and wine are offered in thanksgiving for the gifts of the earth and the gift of Jesus.

4. As a Community Celebration Meal

The Mass is the holy meal of God's people who share Jesus, the bread of life, in Holy Communion. The Eucharist is the food for eternal life. People usually celebrate any important event in their lives with a meal. The Mass is a foretaste of the heavenly banquet where God's people will be united with God.

Related Issues

Attendance at Mass does not, on its own, make someone a good Catholic. People must live in the spirit of the Mass. They have responsibilities beyond the church door. What some of these responsibilities are, and how they can be met, are looked at in this section.

The Body of Christ

St Paul describes the Church as the Body of Christ. Catholics are parts of this Body and must work together to make the Body function properly.

The Mass should have an effect on a Catholic's way of life. At the end of the celebration the priest says, 'Go in peace to love and serve the Lord', so the Catholic has responsibilities to contribute towards the community life of the parish, to pray for the Church, to act to help the poor, and to be friendly with God's people, offering support where it is needed.

In the Parable of the Sheep and the Goats (Matthew 25,31-40), Jesus tells us that we shall be judged at the end of the world by how we have responded to the needs of others. Christ is present in everyone and we should treat everyone as if they were Christ. If we do not respond to people's needs, we shall not go to Heaven.

World Problems

Many thousands of people starve to death annually in the developing countries because there is insufficient food. Over-population adds to this problematic situation. Medical facilities are poor, so many people die of avoidable diseases. Poverty is the underlying factor in all these problems. (See also Chapter 13: The Distribution of Wealth in the World.)

Catholics must respond to such problems, to the needs of the poor, in the spirit of the Mass. They should understand the underlying causes and act to change things. Some of the causes are:

- **Natural disasters.** Floods and droughts make it more difficult, if not impossible, for the poor to work their land. They cannot produce enough food, so they starve.
- **Cycle of debt.** Poor countries are lent money by the developed countries to help them recover from disasters, but they are unable to pay the crippling interest and so are constantly in debt.
- **Unjust trading.** The developed countries' demands for certain crops, e.g. rice, often means that poor countries are producing food for rich countries and not for themselves. The people are not paid a fair return and the land loses its fertility and is ruined for future growth.
- **Poor education.** The people do not know the most efficient agricultural methods and there are no learning facilities for them. Also, they have no money to buy or repair agricultural machinery.
- **Poor medical facilities.** Because of lack of money and education, developing countries are not equipped to deal with disease, and many people die. Poor nutrition and pollution add to this problem.
- **War.** Money is spent on weapons instead of on food. The Western countries are partly to blame because they sell arms to developing countries.
- **Over-population.** Where there is poverty there is often over-population. This is because people are the only resource a poor country may have, to look after its elderly and to help build a community. In addition, there is a high death rate among children in developing countries. Ignorance of family planning is also a factor in over-population.
- **Poor distribution of resources.** Even in the developing countries, a few people are very rich while the majority are very poor.

From these causes, it can be seen that the developed countries are often directly responsible for the poverty in the Third World.

Charity and Aid

Christians can respond to the needs of the poor by prayer and direct action. Few people have the talents or are called to work as missionaries (as nurses, doctors, teachers, farmers, carpenters) in the developing countries, but everyone can help by sharing what they have – giving money to those in need, perhaps by making sacrifices themselves (such as fasting and giving the money to charity).

There are many charities which help the poor overseas. In Britain, the Catholic Fund for Overseas Development (CAFOD) is the official agency of the Catholic Church for overseas development. It is part of Caritas Internationalis. CAFOD began in 1962 with the aim of bringing together all small charitable efforts, to channel money abroad and to promote family fast days.

CAFOD's aim is 'to help people help themselves', to give long-term support, not just food. Every CAFOD project helps local poor people, whatever their colour, religion or nationality, and tries to change the conditions which make people poor. The kind of projects CAFOD supports are: providing clean water and health care; teaching technical skills; developing communities; producing food; and adult and vocational education.

CAFOD provides the structure which enables Catholics to meet their responsibilities to the poor.

20 | Reconciliation

Other terms used for the sacrament of reconciliation are penance and confession, but reconciliation is the preferred term because it expresses more about the meaning of the sacrament.

All people sin and need to be *reconciled* (make friends again) with God and the community. The sacrament is one of healing relationships. It can be celebrated whenever a person feels it is needed. The Church suggests that Roman Catholics should receive the sacrament at least twice a year, during Advent and Lent, to prepare for the major festivals of Christmas and Easter.

The Rite or Ceremony of Reconciliation

The sacrament is usually celebrated by people individually with a priest, but a community of people may celebrate it together with either individual confession and *absolution* (forgiveness) or a general absolution.

Individual Celebration

People may choose to talk to the priest face to face or anonymously, in which case a screen is used. There are no hard and fast rules about how the sacrament should be celebrated. As long as individuals sincerely confess their sins and penance is given, the sacrament is conferred, but the following rite is suggested as a guideline.

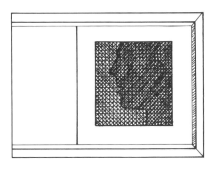

Before going to the priest, the penitent examines his or her conscience and prepares for the sacrament.

- The priest welcomes the penitent.
- A suitable scripture reading is given.
- The penitent confesses his or her sins and the priest offers advice.
- A suitable penance is given.
- The *act of contrition* is said by the penitent, expressing his or her sorrow for sinning and asking for forgiveness.
- The priest gives absolution with his hands extended and makes the sign of the cross over the penitent.
- The penitent says a prayer of praise and thanksgiving, and a final blessing is given by the priest.

Community Celebration with Individual Confession and Absolution

Many priests are needed to celebrate the sacrament in this way. A typical ceremony would be:

- Perhaps a hymn followed by a Liturgy of the Word.
- A homily followed by an examination of conscience.
- A general prayer of confession.
- Another hymn or prayer expressing sorrow for sin, followed by the Lord's Prayer.
- Individual confession of sin.
- Individual absolution.
- Community thanksgiving and a final blessing.

Community Celebration with General Absolution

This may be celebrated when there are insufficient priests to hear individual confessions, and when the need arises. Permission is given by the bishop.

The ceremony is similar to that above. People are advised that if they have committed any serious sins, they must intend to confess them when individual confession is possible.

A general penance is given. People who want absolution signify this in some way, and say together a prayer of confession followed by a prayer or hymn expressing sorrow for sin, and the Lord's Prayer. A general absolution is given, a prayer of thanksgiving is said and a blessing given.

Meaning and Symbolism

Roman Catholics celebrate the sacrament of reconciliation because they understand the necessity to be reconciled to God and the community. All people are sinners, no one is perfect. Catholics must recognise this and in trying to follow Christ faithfully, need forgiveness from him – just as we all do from each other when our human relationships falter. Many Christians pray to God directly, asking for forgiveness, but Catholics believe this is sometimes insufficient. They believe that priests have the power to forgive sins (Matthew 18,18). The priest is the mediator between God and mankind. He represents both God and the community, which has been hurt or damaged by sin.

To understand fully the meaning of the sacrament, the concepts of sin and forgiveness need to be understood, as well as the four main stages in the sacrament itself.

Sin

All people commit sin. The Old Testament word for sin is 'hata' which means 'to miss the mark'. It refers to our failure to reach the goal set us by God, which is to be perfect as our Heavenly Father is perfect. Sin can be a thought or an action, but it can also be a failure to act.

Sin shows itself in us in two ways.

1. Original sin. The story of the Fall in Genesis illustrates the truth that mankind has a tendency to turn away from God. This tendency is termed original sin. We cannot rid ourselves of it by our own efforts and need the healing power of Jesus. In baptism, original sin is overcome.

2. Personal sin. There are two kinds of personal sin:

a) *Mortal sins.* These are very serious sins which result in death to the Life of Christ within us. The sinner knows that what he or she is doing is very wrong and yet consciously chooses to do it. It is not necessarily the act which makes a sin mortal, but the intention behind it – for example, killing someone may not be a mortal sin if it is an accident. Mortal sins can be forgiven only in the sacrament of reconciliation with perfect contrition, or in martyrdom.

b) *Venial sins.* These are less serious sins which give a bad example, such as making a nasty remark. Venial sins can be forgiven through personal prayer, but they can build up and begin to affect the person's character and should therefore be confessed in the sacrament of reconciliation.

Forgiveness

All people need forgiveness. Sin damages the individual, the community and the individual's relationship with God. In the sacrament of reconciliation, the penitent experiences the healing touch of Christ and is made whole again. He or she receives the grace to make a new start, to become a more loving person. In the New Testament, Jesus forgives sinners on many occasions – for example, Zacchaeus, the tax collector (Luke 19,1-10), the woman taken in adultery (Luke 7,36-50). The parable of the lost son (Luke 15,11-32) illustrates how God forgives the repentant sinner.

Stages in the Sacrament

1. Contrition is the change of heart by which the penitent allows God to convert him/her (sorrow for having sinned).

2. Confession is the opening of one's heart to the priest and telling him one's sins.

3. Satisfaction is when the penitent tries to make some recompense for sin. The penance can be prayer, fasting, almsgiving or actions to help others.

4. Absolution is forgiveness of sin by the priest through the power of the Holy Spirit. Sin cannot be forgiven unless the penitent is truly sorry. God knows what is in the heart.

Related Issues

Reconciliation in society is needed in three main areas: crime and punishment; prejudice and discrimination; war and peace.

Crime and Punishment (See also Chapter 10)

A crime is a social act which offends the laws of society. Societies have laws and when these are broken the offender is a criminal. There are many causes of crime, such as greed, unemployment, boredom, poverty, revenge, drugs and media influence.

Laws are necessary in society for the good of everyone. The law defines what is criminal and the courts decide suitable punishments. There are different types of court to deal with different kinds of crime.

Punishments vary tremendously, and include probation, attendance centres, community service, fines, imprisonment. Capital punishment and corporal punishment are not allowed in Britain at present. Capital punishment is the death sentence. Corporal punishments are physical forms, e.g. the birch or mutilation of a limb.

Four main aims of punishment can be identified:

1. Deterrence – to deter (put off) the criminal and others from committing crime.

2. Protection – to protect society from the criminal. For example, a thief in prison cannot thieve.

3. Revenge – to make the criminal pay so that society feels avenged.

4. Reform – to help criminals understand that their crimes were wrong, so they will resolve not to commit crime again and can be rehabilitated into society.

Christians consider that punishment is necessary for the good of society – to protect the community and to deter the criminal. As is reflected in the sacrament of reconciliation, the criminal must admit his or her crime (confession) and make recompense (penance). The reformative aim is the most important, as criminals must feel sorrow for their wrongdoing (contrition) and resolve not to commit crime again. Society can then forgive criminals (absolution) as they are rehabilitated into society. Many Christians do not agree with the revenge aim of punishment.

Jesus's teaching on this issue can be found in the following references: Matthew 5,12-26, 5,38-42 and 5,43-48, and Luke 15,11-32. St. Paul also gives advice on the treatment of the criminal in his letter to Philemon.

Prejudice and Discrimination (See also Chapter 12)

Prejudice occurs when people prejudge others because of their colour, race, sex, class, age or religion, and dislike them because of it. Discrimination occurs when a person or group is treated differently because of prejudice. Prejudiced people may discriminate against others by, for example, choosing not to employ someone because of the colour of his or her skin. The main forms of discrimination arise from racial and sexual inequality, mental or physical handicap, and the generation gap.

Jesus was never prejudiced and never discriminated against anyone. He welcomed society's outcasts with open arms. The outcasts in the New Testament were lepers, tax collectors, prostitutes, Romans and Samaritans. See the following stories for evidence of Jesus's acceptance of these people: lepers – Luke 17,11-19; tax collectors – Luke 19,1-10; prostitutes – Luke 7,36-50; Romans – Luke 7,1-20; Samaritans – Luke 10,25-37. Jesus shows that Christians should not show prejudice or discrimination.

The sacrament of reconciliation can help people overcome their prejudice and begin to build better relationships.

War and Peace (See also Chapter 14)

War is common in our society and the causes may be quite complicated. They include defence of a nation, revenge, greed for power, injustice and poverty.

The Christian Church teaches that certain conditions must be met before a war can be considered justifiable (legally or morally justified). This is the 'just war' theory.

- The war must be waged by a legitimate authority.
- There should be a reasonable chance of success.
- War should only be a last resort.
- The cause must be serious enough to justify the suffering.
- The right intention is necessary to bring about justice and peace.
- Methods used should be morally legitimate so that innocent civilians are not killed, and the good achieved must outweigh the evil done.

It is very difficult to meet all the conditions necessary for a just war, and it can be argued that no war in history has been completely justified with the exception perhaps of World War Two.

It is argued that no nuclear war or use of chemical weapons could ever be justified, because it would result in vast destruction and in the killing of millions of innocent people.

Christians, therefore, should be concerned to see the disarmament of nuclear weapons and the banning of chemical weapons. Some Christians argue that nuclear weapons are necessary as a deterrent to the enemy, but would agree that there are many more weapons than are necessary and there should therefore be some disarmament. Others say it is immoral to spend money on weapons while people are starving and the education and health of people is suffering.

The Church teaches that disarmament is desirable. There are two ways of disarmament and Christians can support either way.

1. Unilateral – one nation has the courage to withdraw all its weapons independently, as an example to others.

2. Multilateral – the most powerful nations gradually reduce arms equally by agreement.

War is caused by breakdowns in relationships between nations. Nations need to be reconciled to each other, as is reflected in the sacrament of reconciliation. They must recognise that these international tensions are wrong and must honestly propose to rebuild relationships and make practical moves towards nuclear disarmament.

Jesus taught of justice and peace and of loving our enemies (Matthew 5,43-48). Pacifism is suggested, yet he challenged the religious authorities in his day. St. Paul tells us we should obey the State, which derives its authority from God (Romans 13,1-7).

21 Anointing of the Sick

Other names for the sacrament of Anointing of the Sick are the Sacrament of the Sick, the Last Rites and Extreme Unction. In the past the sacrament was linked with forgiveness of sin, and because severe penances were given, people left it until death was imminent. Today, the sacrament may be celebrated at any time the need is felt, not just at the point of death. It may be celebrated in the privacy of an individual's home or within Mass for a number of people.

The Rite or Ceremony of the Anointing of the Sick

1. Greeting and blessing with holy water. The priest explains the sacrament and reads James 5,14-15.

2. Reconciliation. The person may confess his or her sins. This may have been done previously.

3. Reading from scripture and homily.

4. Prayers of intercession are said for the sick person and for those who care for the sick.

5. Laying-on of hands by the priest.

6. A thanksgiving prayer is said for the oil of the sick.

7. Anointing on the forehead and hands with the oil of the sick.

8. A prayer is said, followed by the Lord's Prayer.

9. A blessing is given.

If a person is dying, Holy Communion may also be given (viaticum).

For a group of people the sacrament may be celebrated in a group ceremony or within Mass, usually between the Liturgy of the Word and the Liturgy of the Eucharist.

The sacrament should not be abused and should be received only when there is real need. It may be received many times and may be requested in the following cases:

- If a person is in danger of death through illness or accident.
- If a major operation is about to be performed.
- If a person is elderly and frail (for strength).
- If young children are sick (for comfort).
- If there are unconscious people who would have requested the sacrament if they were able.

Meaning and Symbolism

Anointing of the sick is a sign of comfort, forgiveness and healing. It may have the following effects:

● The sick person receives the strength and courage of the Holy Spirit to accept illness or death. The laying-on of hands and anointing symbolise this.

● The sick person's sins are forgiven (in confession).

● The sick person receives the healing power of the Holy Spirit, which gives spiritual comfort. Some people may recover from their illness.

Related Issues

Sickness and Healing

Sickness and suffering are signs of an imperfect world. They are facts of human existence, but we cannot easily accept sickness, especially in the very young, or when we see loved ones suffering. The Christian can be helped to overcome suffering through the healing power of Jesus. He healed many sick people and continues to do so for those who have faith in him. Pilgrimages of the sick to shrines such as Lourdes have helped tremendously, if not by curing the sick, then by giving them the courage and strength to face the future. Impact is made, too, on the helpers and carers who share in a special communion of love in serving the sick. The sacrament of the sick can also bring great comfort and strength. Jesus continues to heal in the world.

Jesus himself suffered tremendous physical pain and an agonising death, but the great Christian message is that he transformed it through his resurrection. He promised that all who believe will share in the resurrection.

Christians recognise that through suffering comes redemption. Sickness brings great trauma and challenge, but can be an occasion of great spiritual growth for the patient and his or her family. It can help relationships to deepen, as the sick person needs to depend on the love and support of family and friends. Sickness and suffering, when joined with Christ's, can be a power to help bring the love of God into the world. It can help people to appreciate the need for God's love and to understand the weaknesses of others. Suffering should not be sought, however, as it can bring despair to the unbeliever and tests relationships with God and others.

The sick have worth and dignity. All Christians should respond to their needs with love, care and respect, offering support and encouragement. The hospice movement was developed to provide this sort of support, as well as to provide expert medical care for the terminally ill.

Euthanasia (see also Chapter 11) occurs when the death of someone is hastened. It is sometimes called mercy-killing, because it often refers to the terminally ill or very elderly. Some people support voluntary euthanasia, arguing that individuals have the right to decide their own death. Compulsory euthanasia was practised in World War Two by the Nazis on mentally or physically handicapped people. Christianity teaches that life is a gift from God, so only God has the right to take life, but it also teaches that people should be allowed to die naturally and should not be kept alive at all costs.